Rowena V. Dagdag
Aileen O. Ruivivar

Authors

Art Skills Builder

ISBN: 978-971-625-410-5

First RVC Building, 92 Anonas Cor. K-6th Streets,
East Kamias, Quezon City

Tel. Nos: (02) 8426-5611 | (02) 8573-2380

Telefax No.: (02) 8426-1274

Email: inquiry@stmatthews.ph

Website: www.stmatthews.ph

Note: This book was prepared with the utmost care and scrutiny.

Errors which may be discovered while reading the book will be corrected

in the next printing. The publisher guarantees the replacement

of books received and found to have physical defects like binding

and printing, provided that the defects are found before use.

Just call telephone nos. (02) 8426-1274 or (02) 8426-5611.

The books will be replaced immediately.

Published by **St. Matthew's Publishing Corporation**

NOTE TO PARENTS AND TEACHERS

The *Skills Builder Series* provides you with a helpful tool in letting young learners practice their skills in five subject areas: Reading, Writing, Math, Filipino and Art. The books in the series assist learners in reviewing concepts tackled in each subject. They also offer enrichment activities for learners to achieve mastery of skills.

Each book in the *Skills Builder Series* allows you to follow up on the progress and development of each learner using the Performance Tracker found on the last page of the book.

As parents, guardians or teachers, you are encouraged to accompany the child in his/her learning journey. You may read the instructions to the learner, check accomplished activities together, and answer questions the learner may have about certain activities. Challenge the learner to practice the skills he/she picked up from the Skills Builder books to his/her everyday lives. Guide him/her to be an independent and competent learner.

The *Art Skills Builder* book aims to support the child in the different developmental areas such as language, psycho-motor, cognitive and creative skills. Most importantly the exposure and the experience in Art awaken, enhance and boost the child's academic success.

This book supports and reinforces what young children learn in school. It also expands their imagination and creativity.

Children are born natural artists. Let them be the artists that they are!

TABLE OF CONTENTS

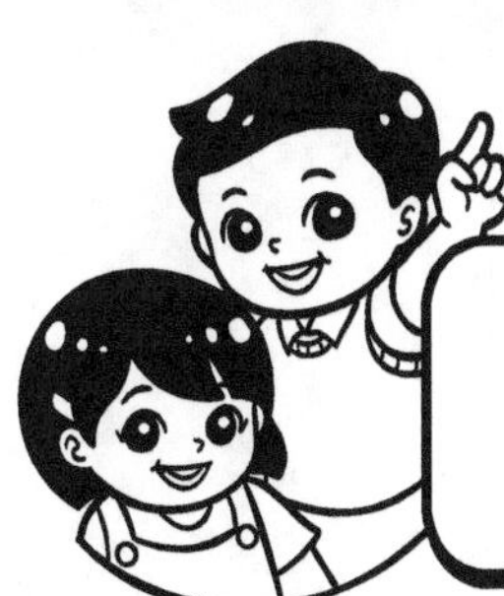

Lines and Strokes

Horizontal Lines

Connect the dots. Color the picture after.

horizontal line

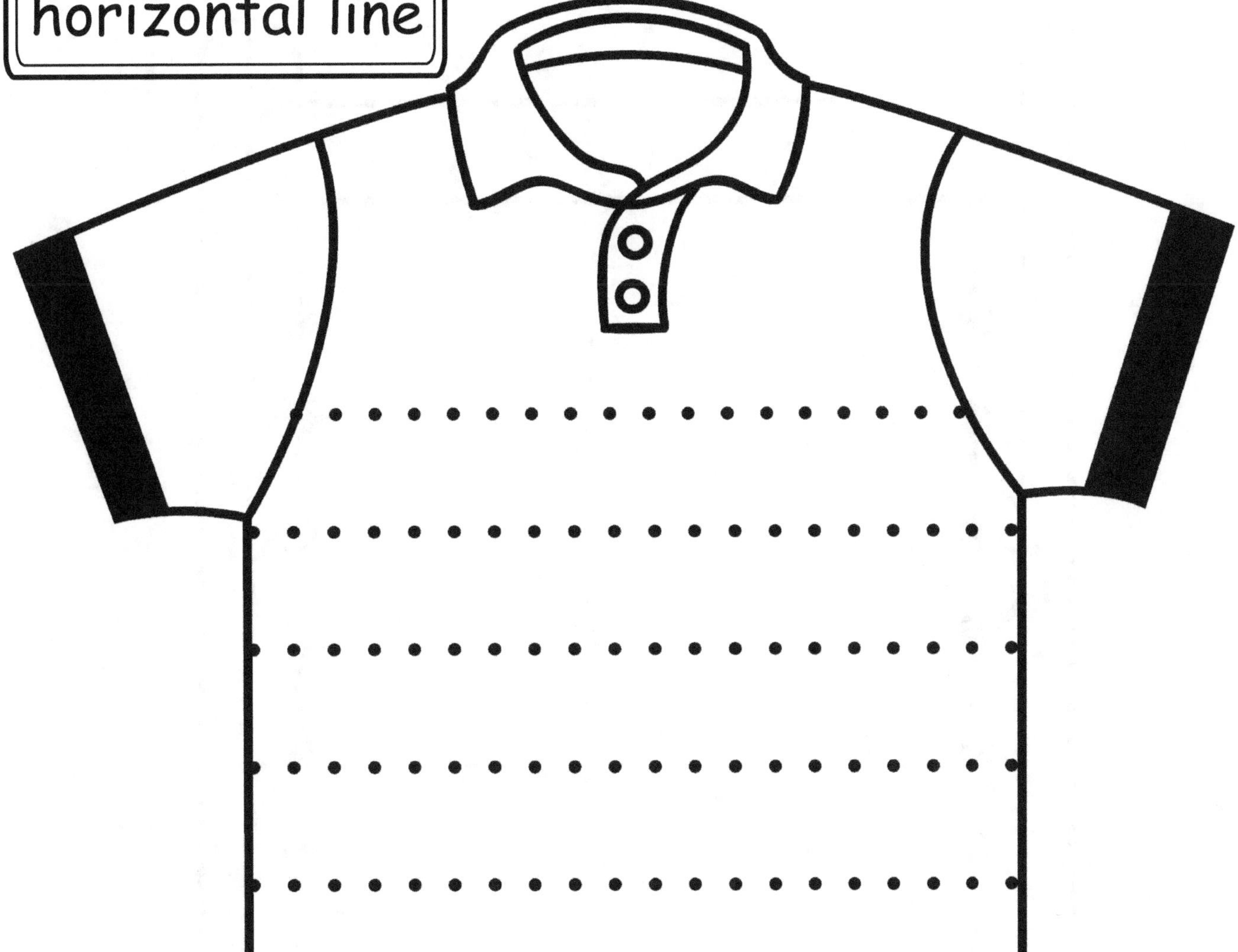

Skills: Prewriting; Coloring; Tracing

Lines and Strokes

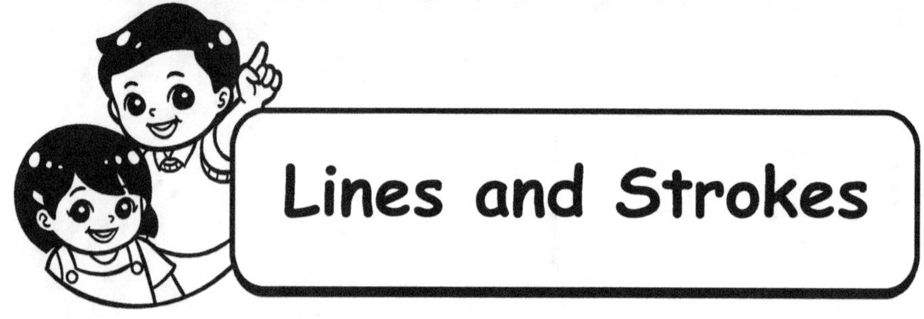

Horizontal Lines

Draw horizontal lines to complete the ladder. Color the picture after.

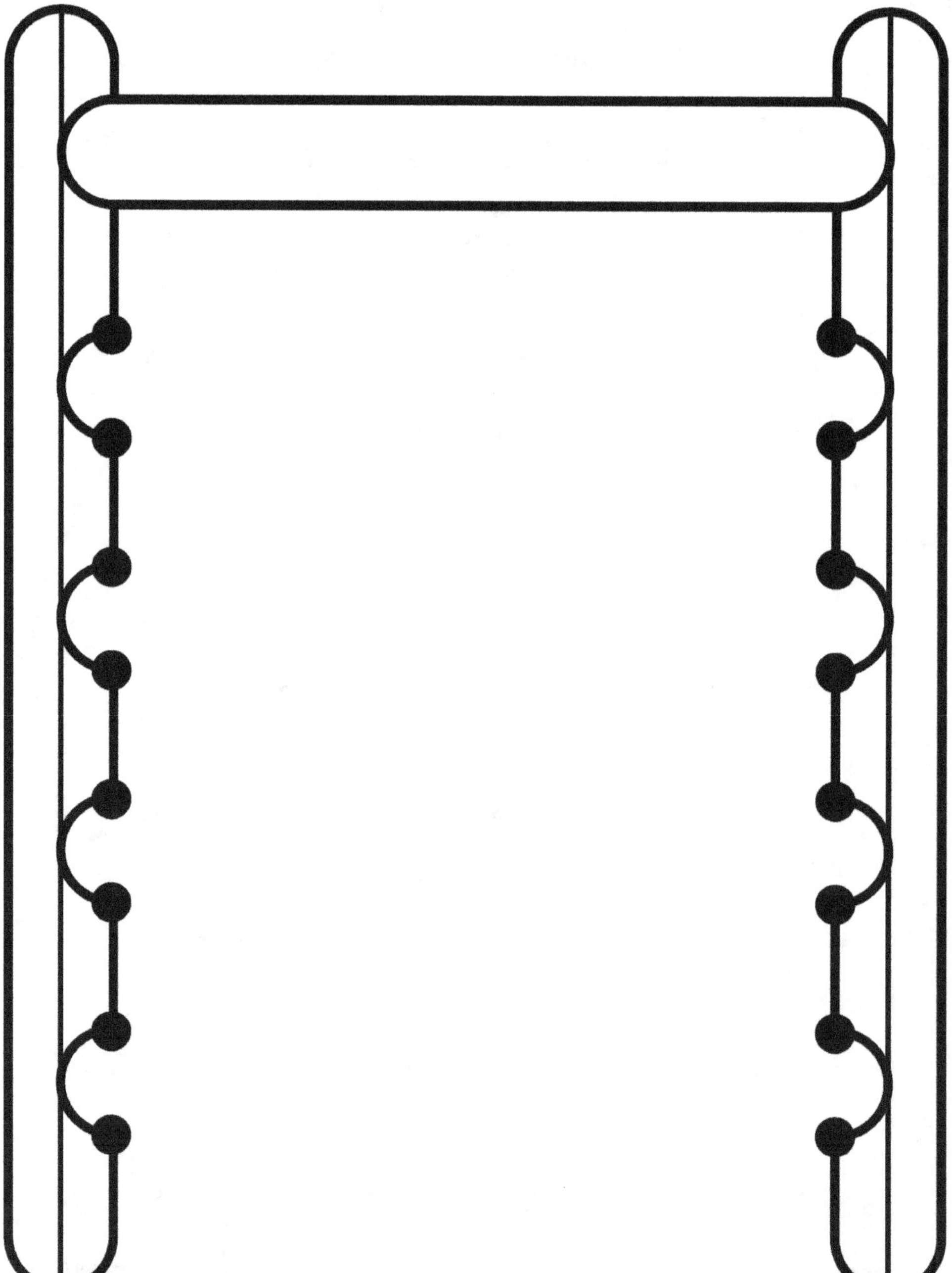

Skills: Drawing; Coloring

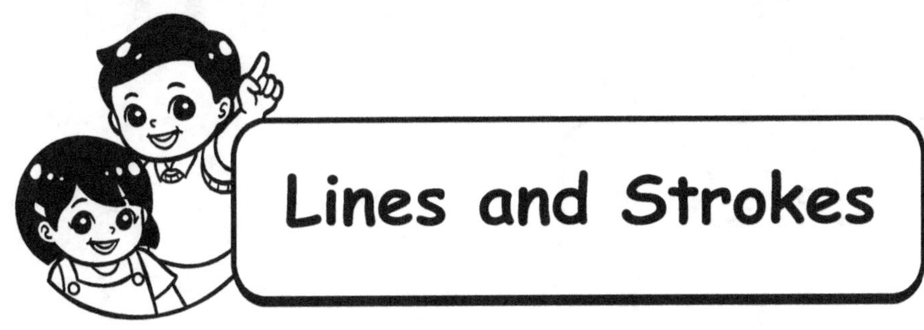

Lines and Strokes

Vertical Lines

Draw vertical lines to complete the gate. Color the picture after.

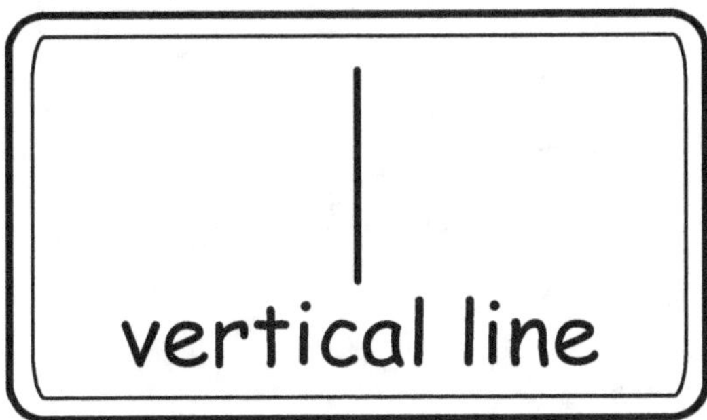

vertical line

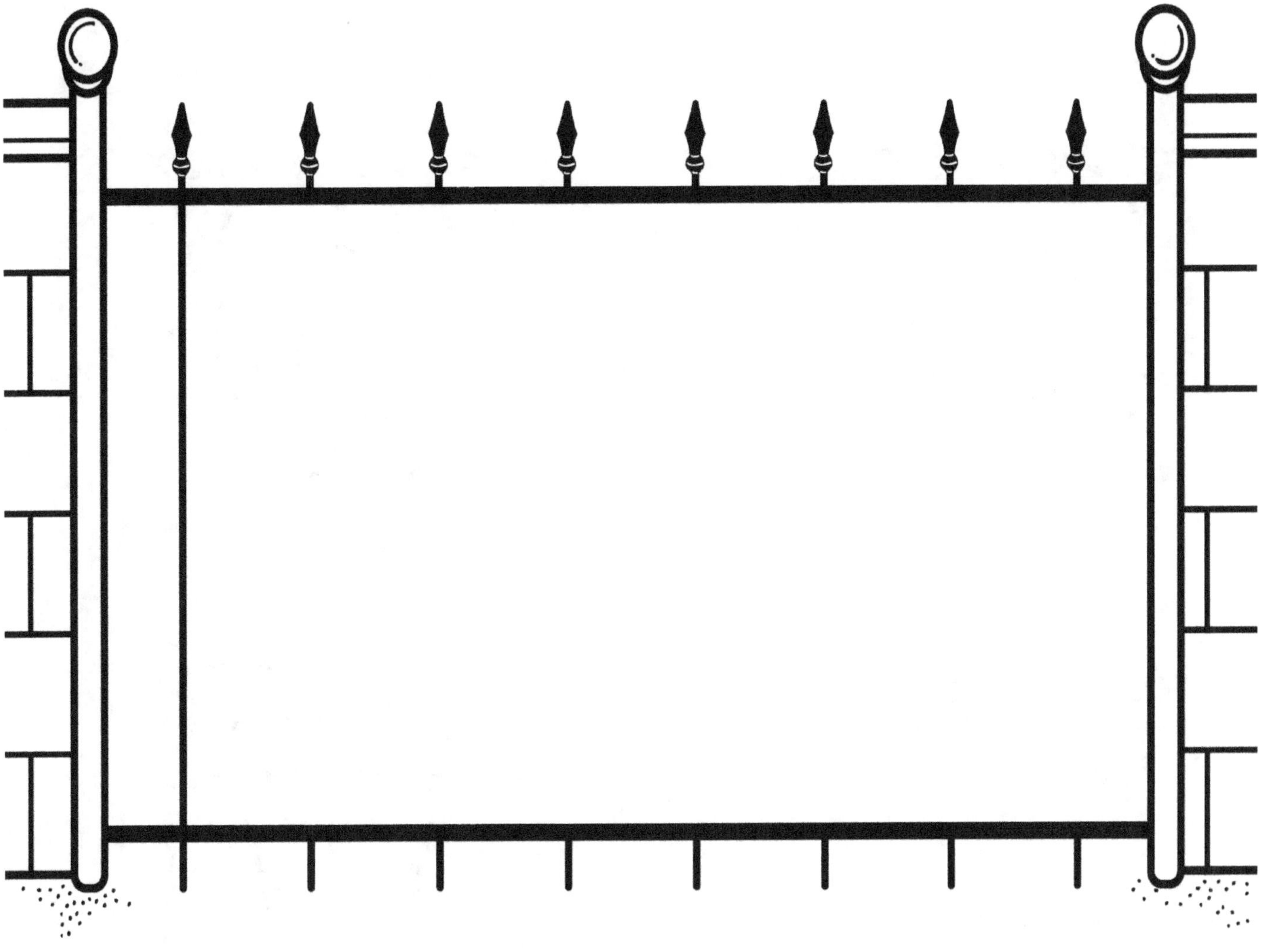

Lines and Strokes

Vertical Lines

Make vertical lines from top to bottom to make stems. Color the pictures after.

4

Skills: Drawing; Coloring

Lines and Strokes

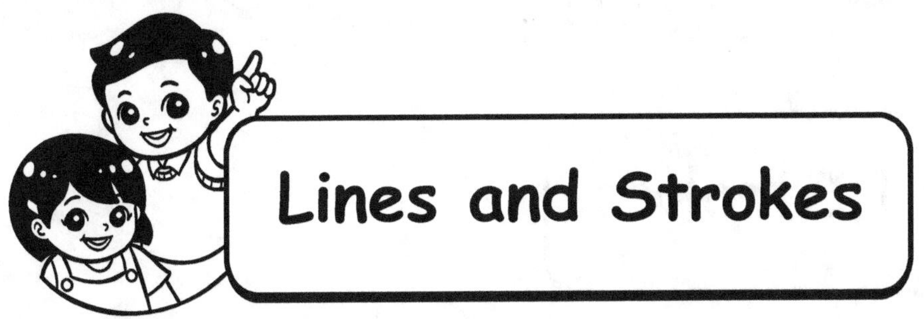

Horizontal and Vertical Lines

Draw horizontal and vertical lines to complete the house. Color the picture after.

Skills: Drawing; Coloring

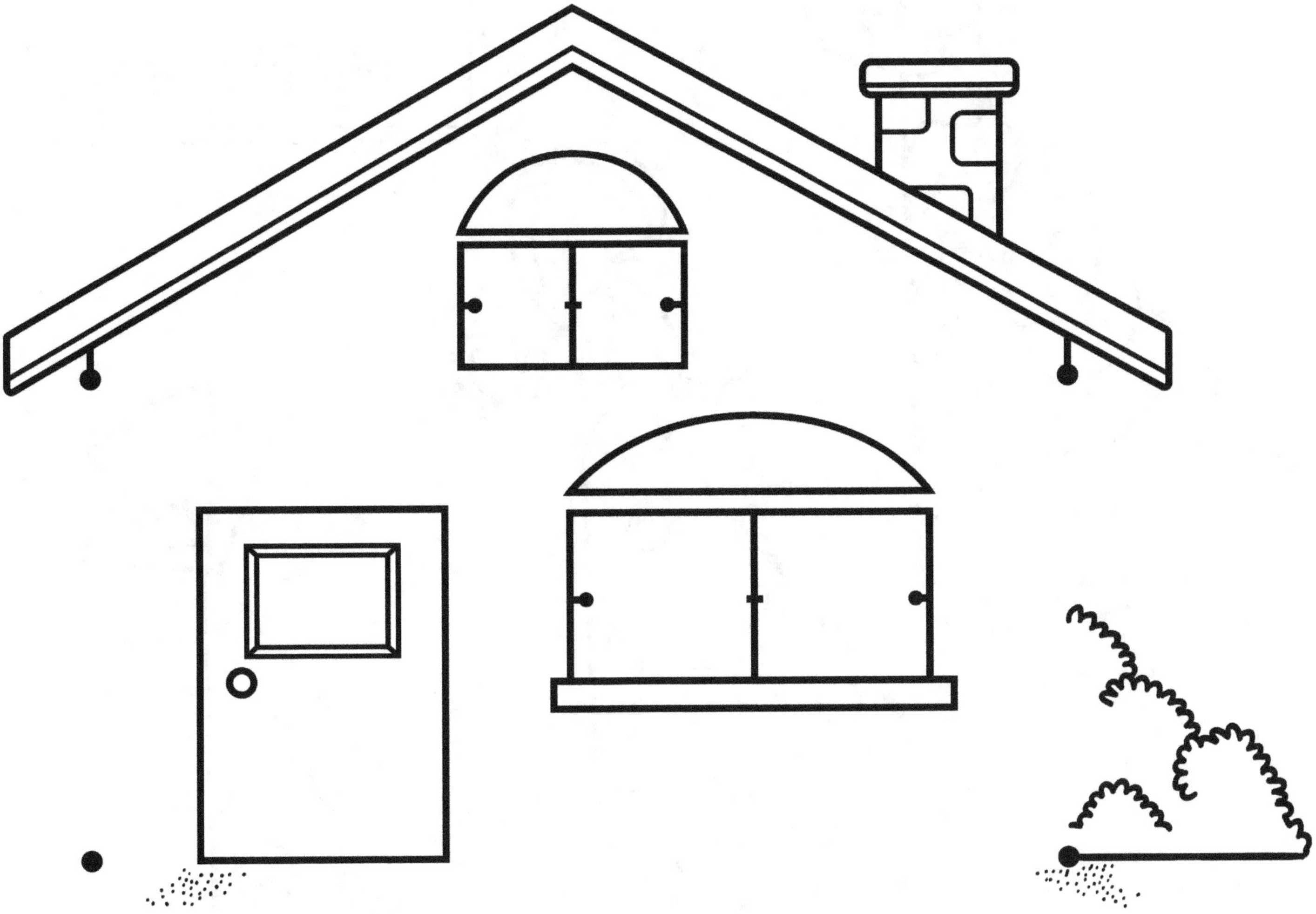

Lines and Strokes

Right Slants

Connect the right slants. Color the picture after.

right slant

Skills: Prewriting; Coloring; Tracing

Right Slants

Draw right slants to make rain. Color the picture after.

Lines and Strokes

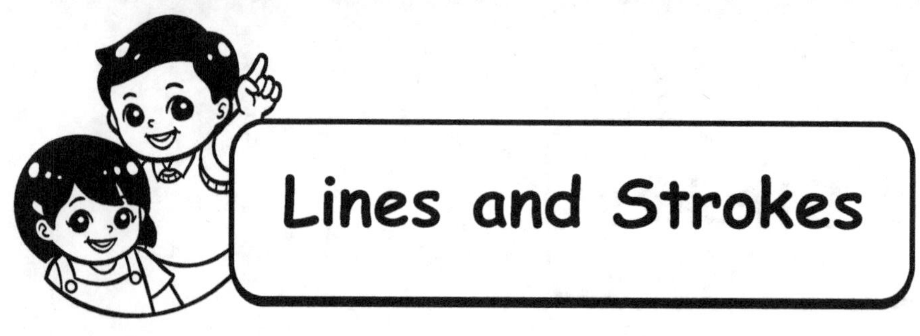

Left Slants

Make left slants by tracing the lines. One is done for you.

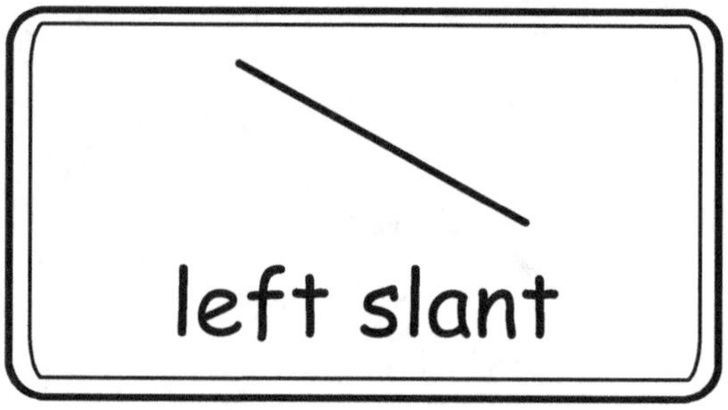

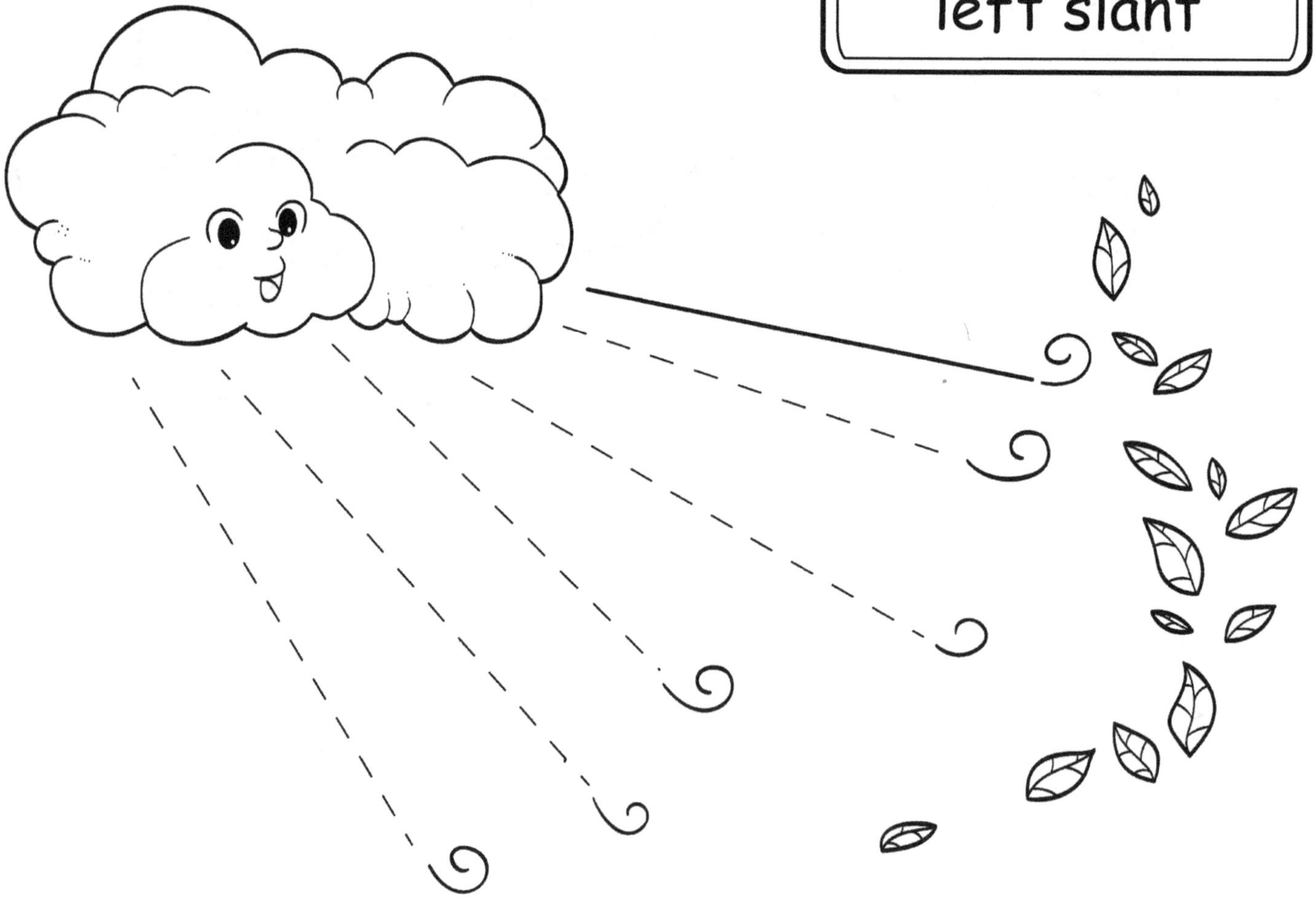

Skills: Prewriting; Tracing

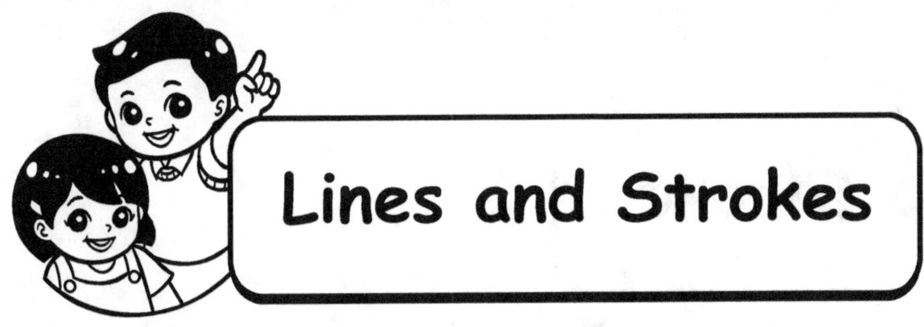

Lines and Strokes

Right and Left Slants

Make right and left slants to make teepees. Color the picture after.

Skills: Drawing; Coloring

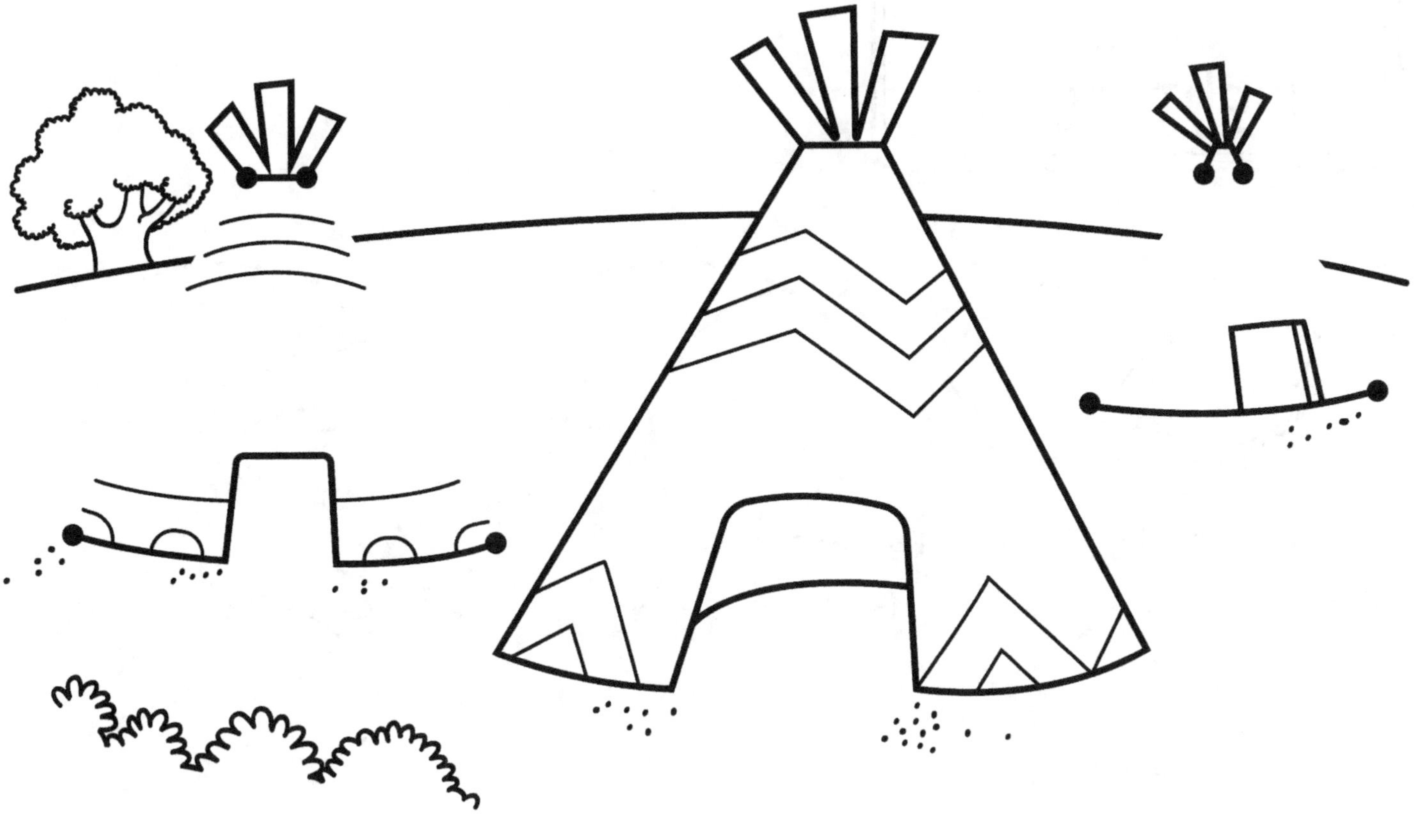

Right Curves

Trace the right curves to complete the picture.

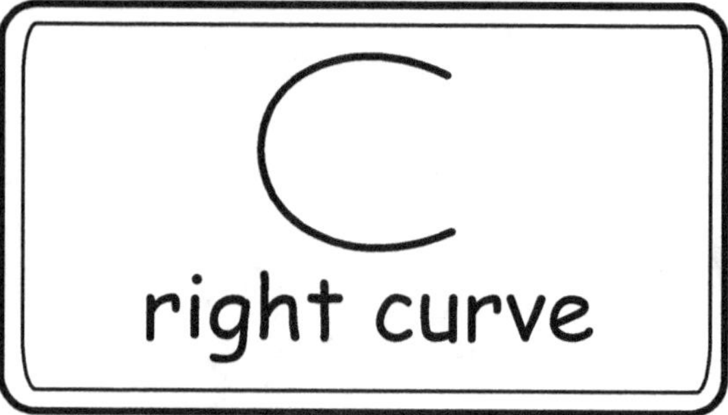

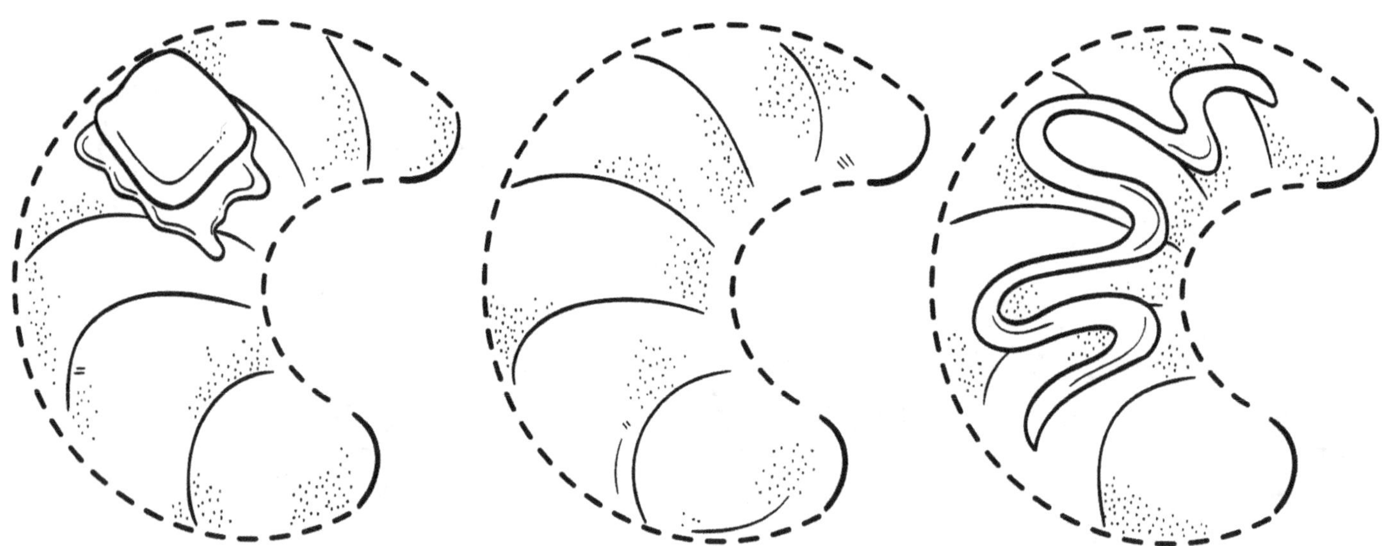

Skills: Prewriting; Tracing

Lines and Strokes

Right Curves

Draw right curves. Color the picture after.

Skills: Drawing; Coloring

Lines and Strokes

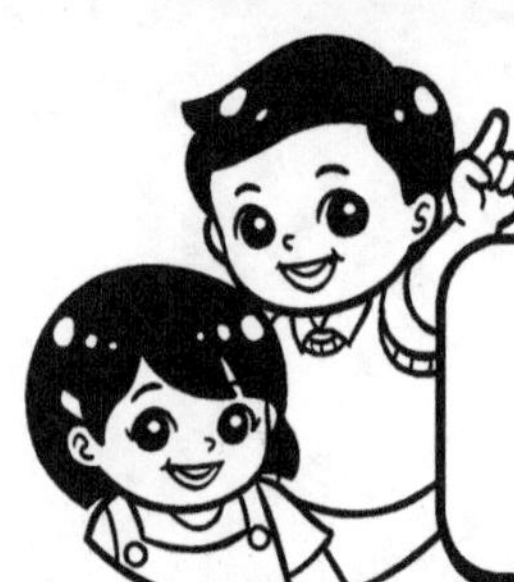

Left Curves

Make left curves. One is done for you.

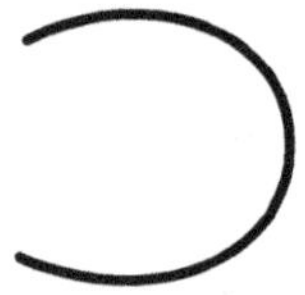

left curve

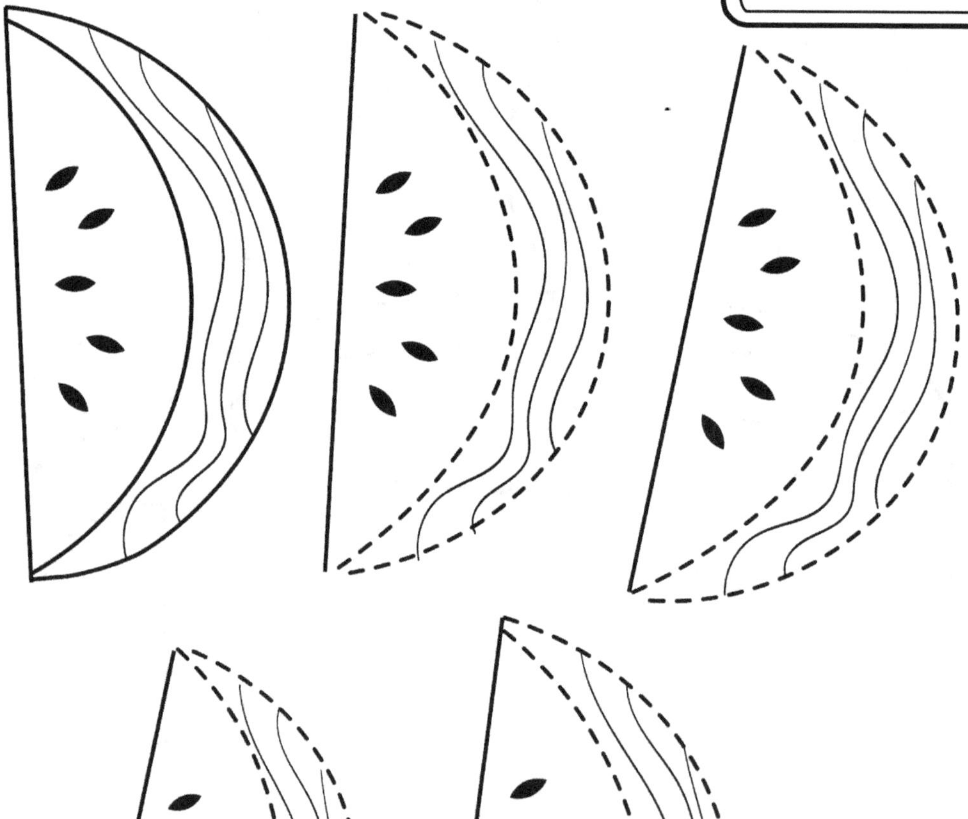

Skills: Prewriting; Tracing

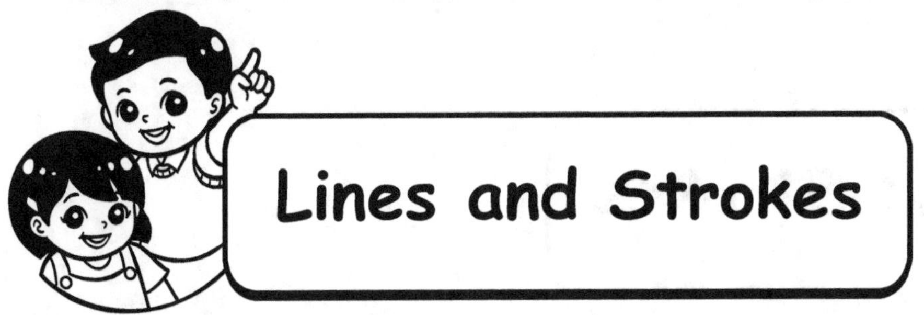

Left Curves

Draw left curves. Color the picture after.

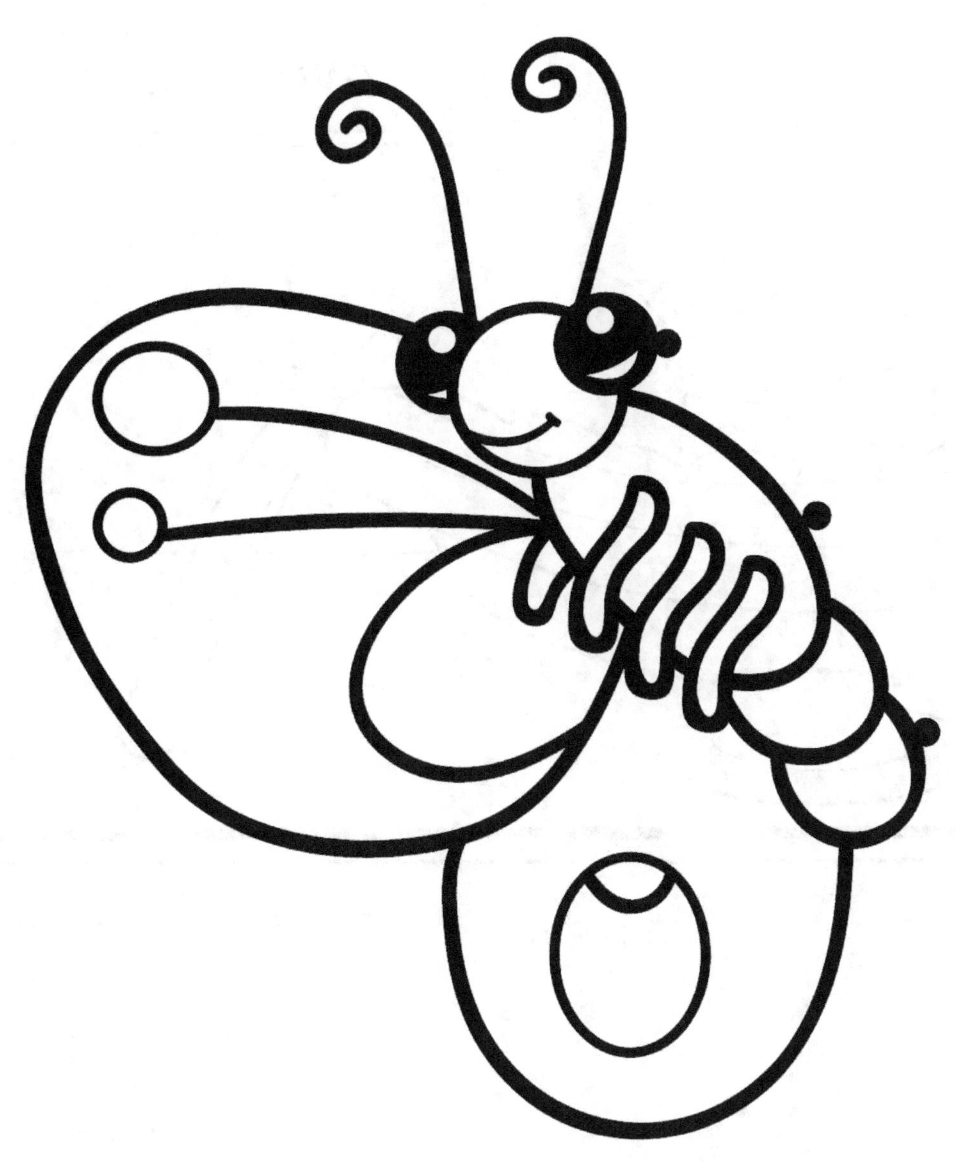

Over Curves

Trace over curve lines and color the picture after.

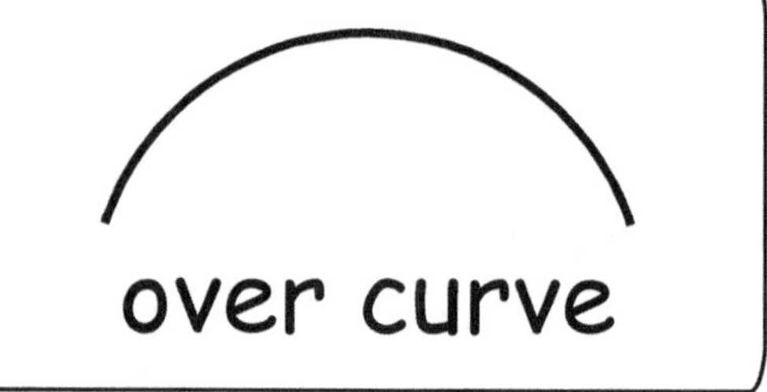

Skills: Prewriting; Tracing; Coloring

Lines and Strokes

Over Curves

Draw over curve lines on the sheep.

Lines and Strokes

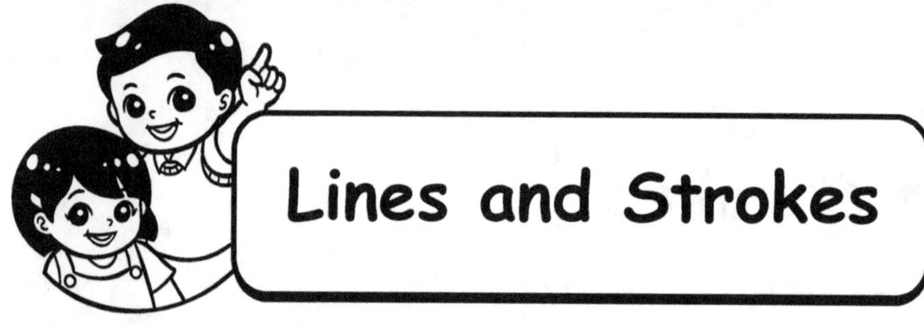

Under Curves

Draw under curves to complete the picture. Color it after.

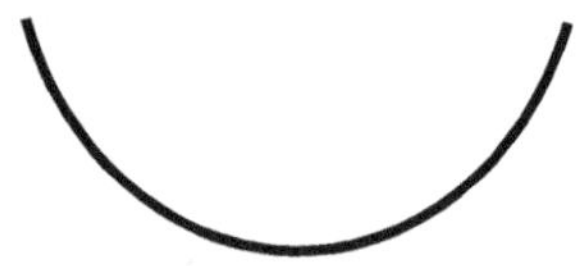

under curve

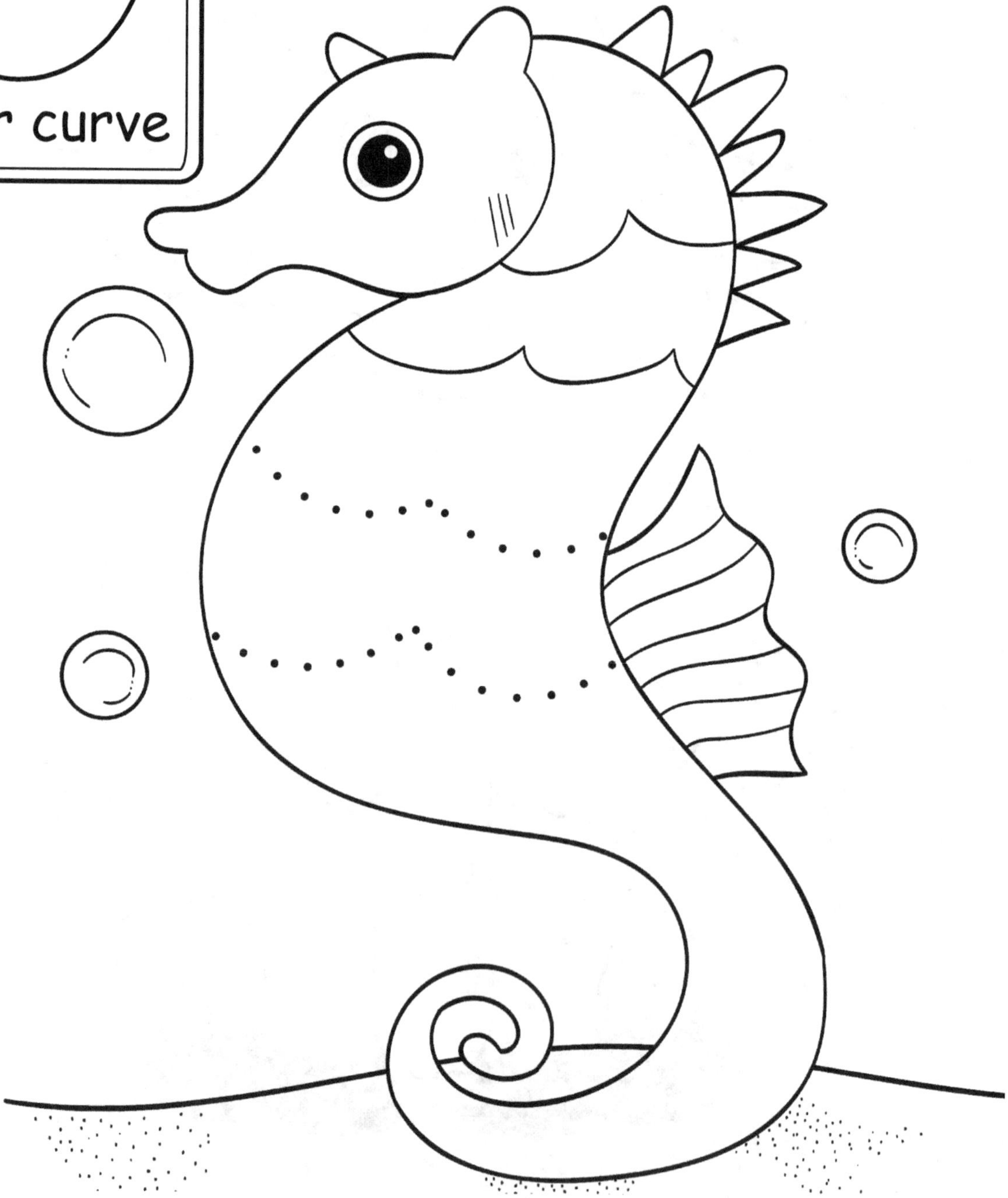

Skills: Prewriting; Drawing; Coloring

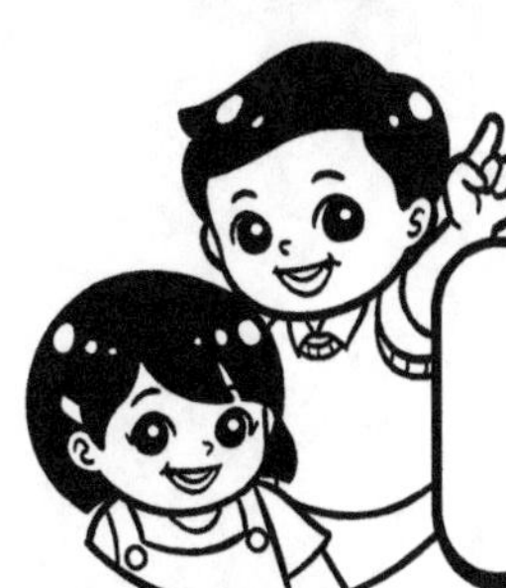

Lines and Strokes

Under Curves

Draw under curves on the tree. Color the picture after.

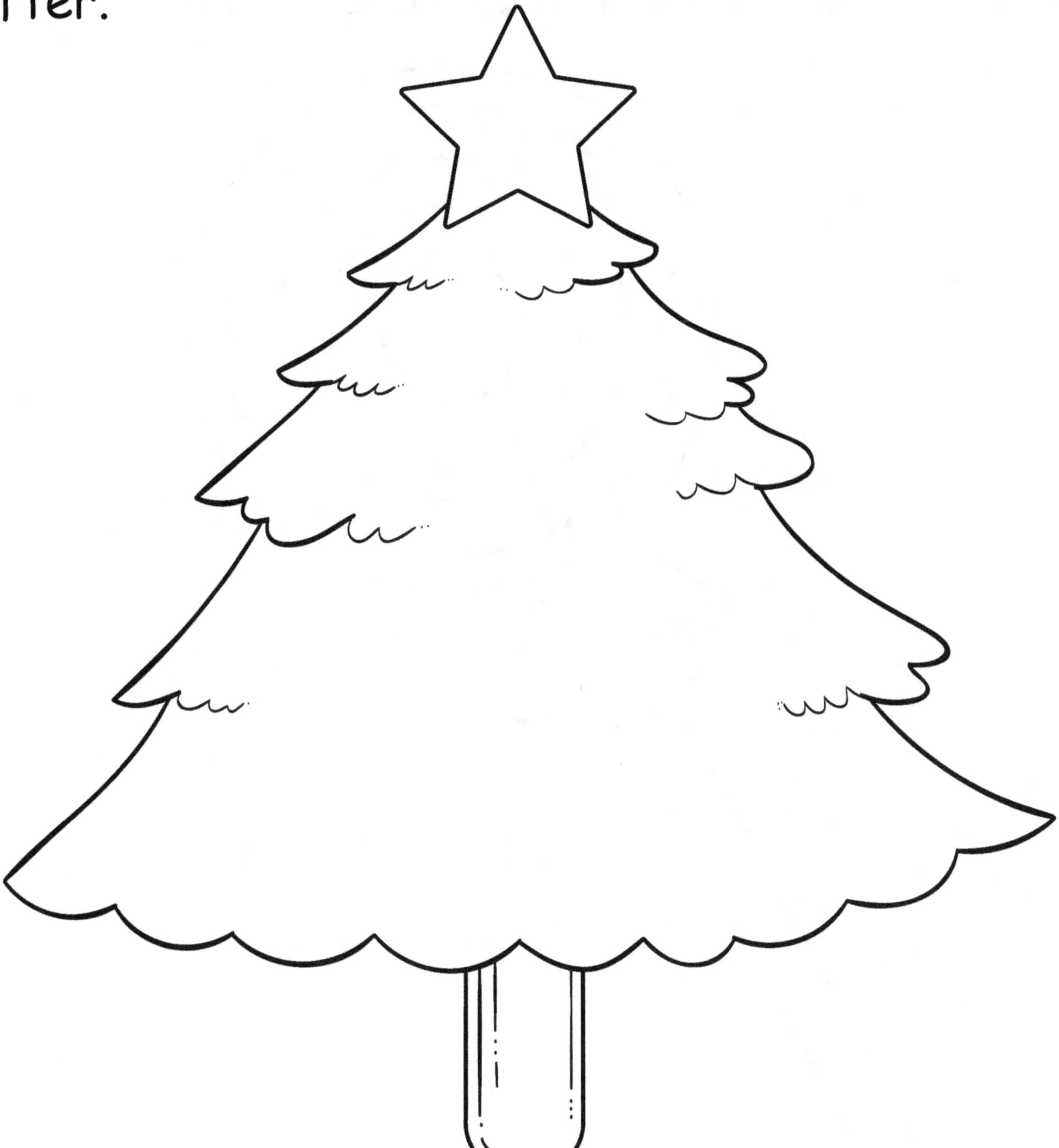

Skills: Drawing; Coloring

Lines and Strokes

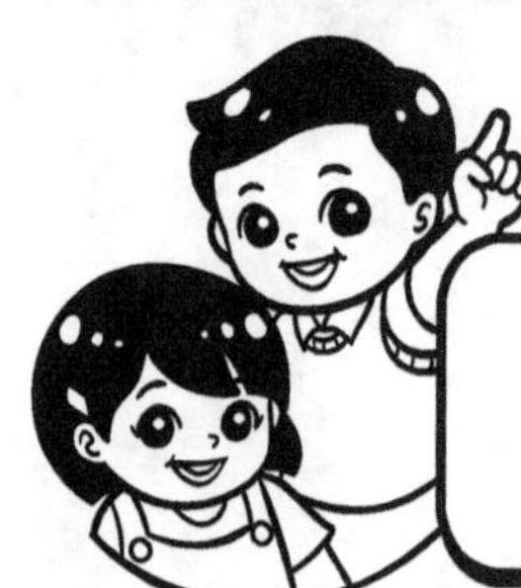

Over and Under Curves

Trace the broken lines to make over and under curves. Color the picture after.

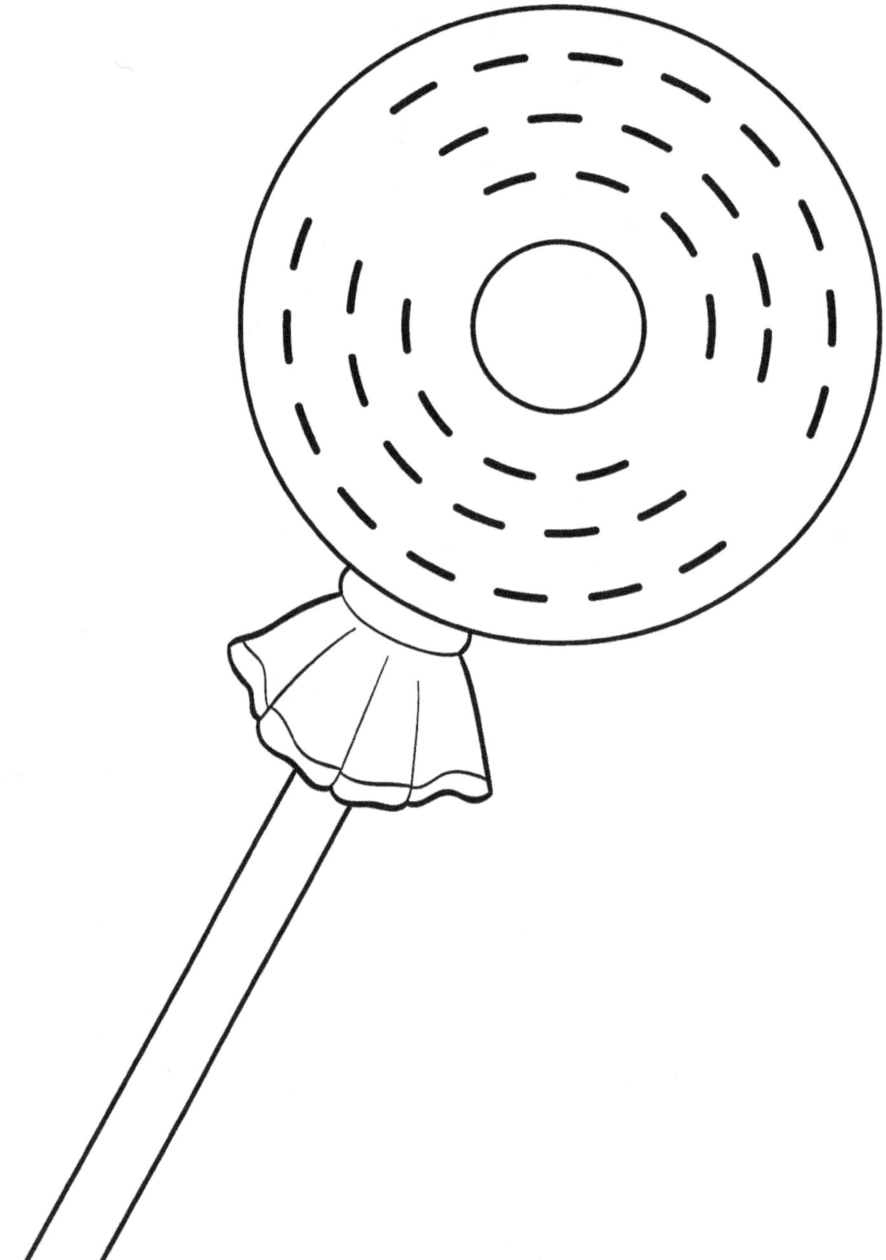

Skills: Tracing; Coloring

Lines and Strokes

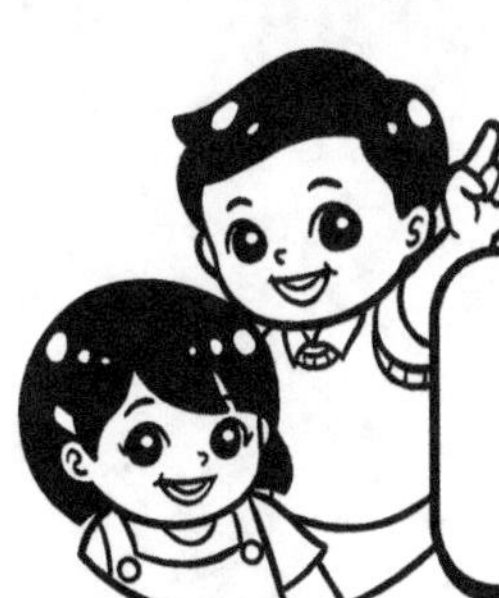

Over and Under Curves

Color the whale and put more waves.

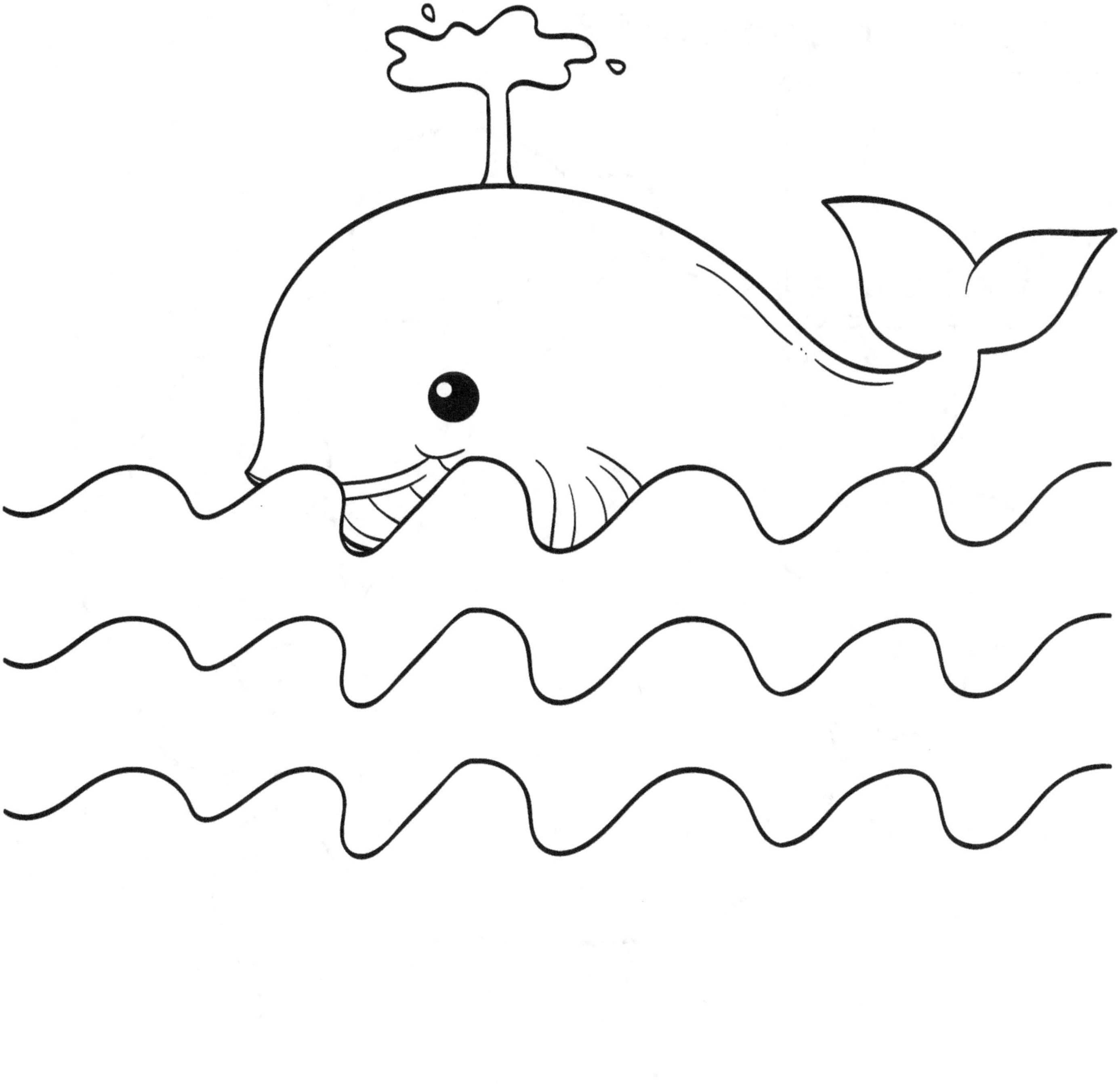

Lines and Strokes

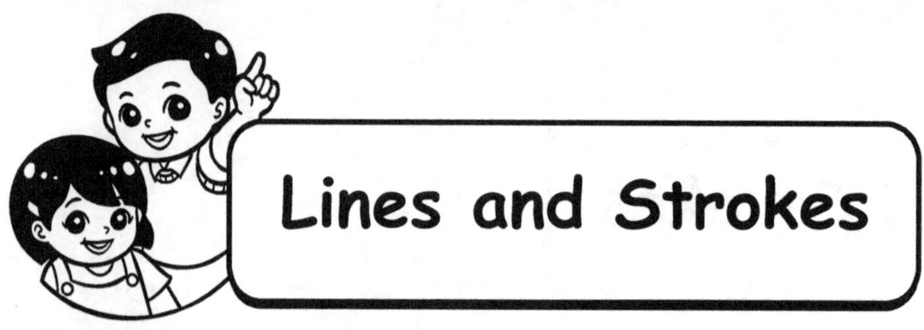

Closed Curves

Draw closed curves to make eyes and a nose. Color the picture after.

closed curve

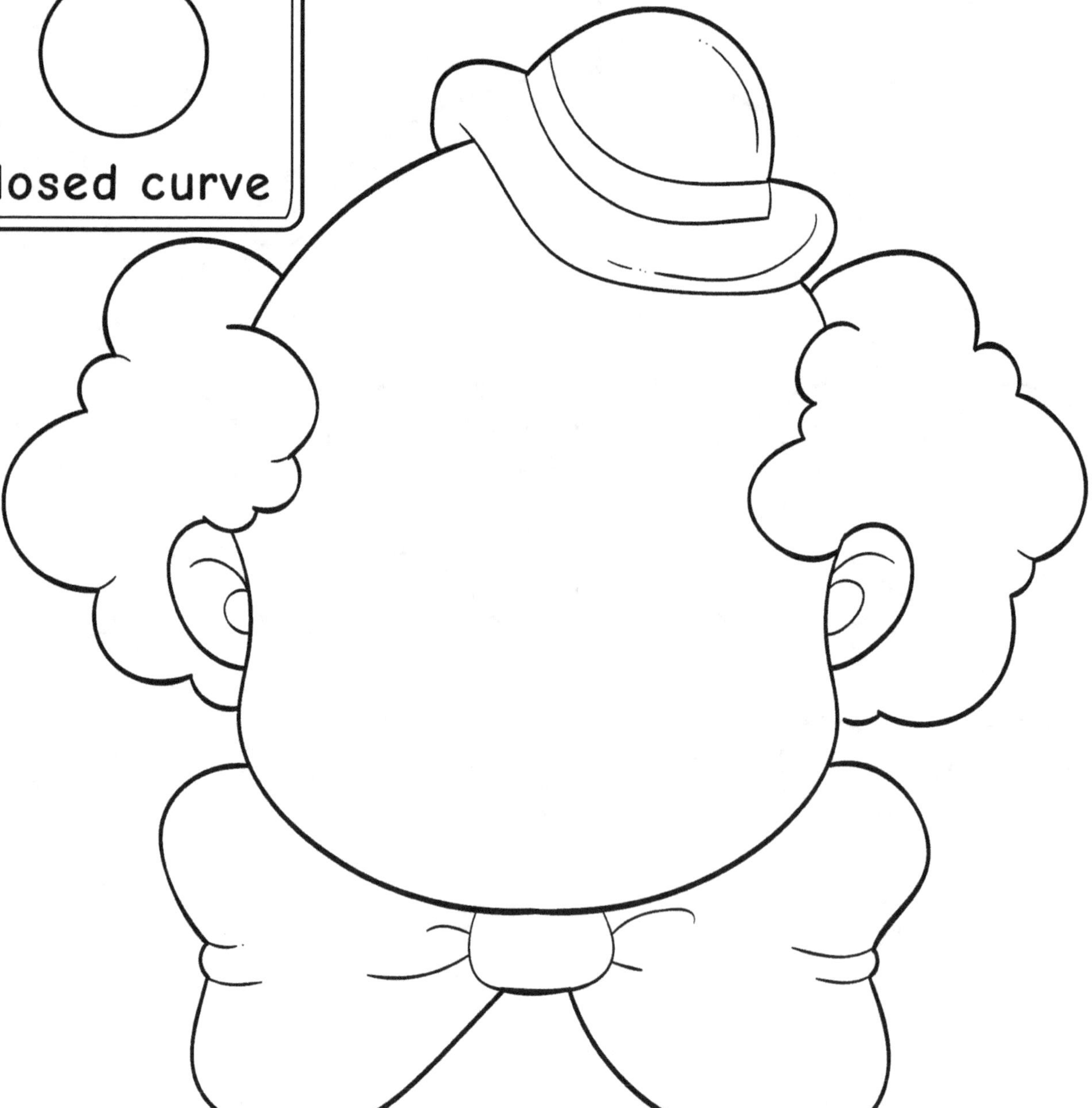

Skills: Drawing; Coloring

Lines and Strokes

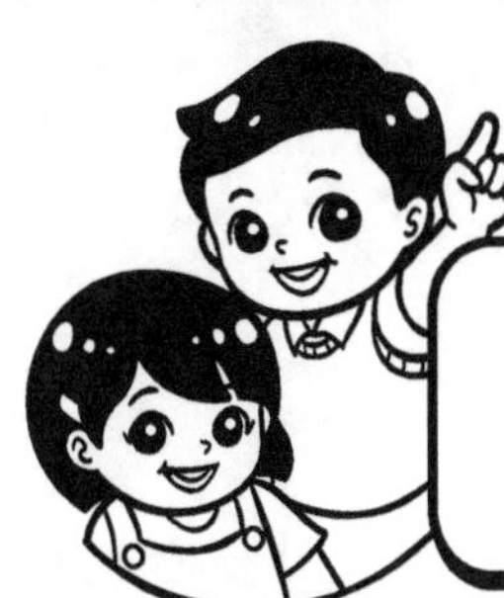

Closed Curves

Draw oranges on the tree. Color the picture after.

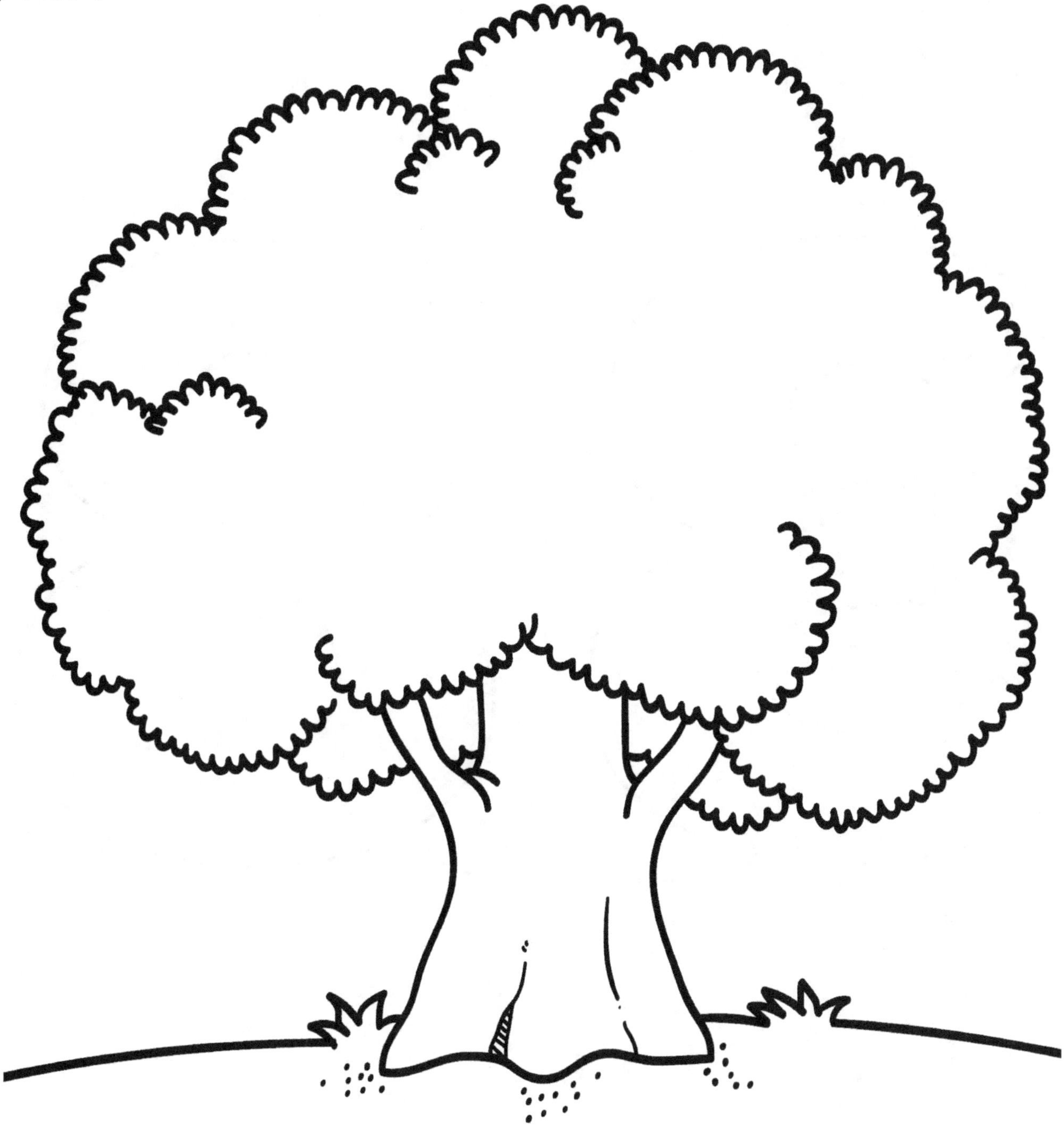

Lines and Strokes

Open and Closed Curves

Write numbers 3 and 8 inside.

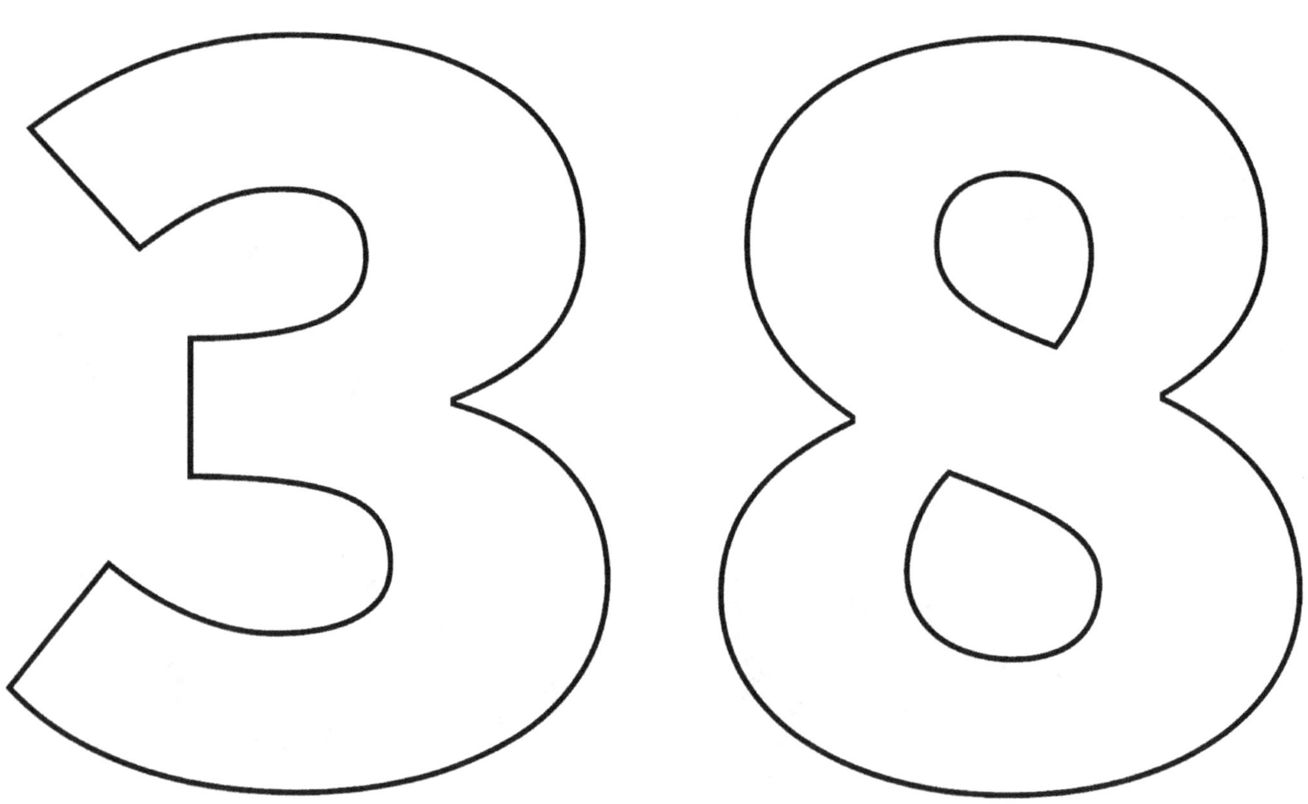

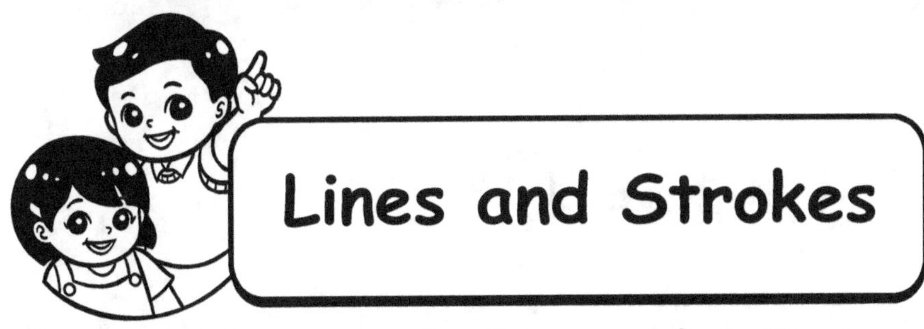

Lines and Strokes

Straight and Curved Lines

Trace number two to make a swan. Color the picture after.

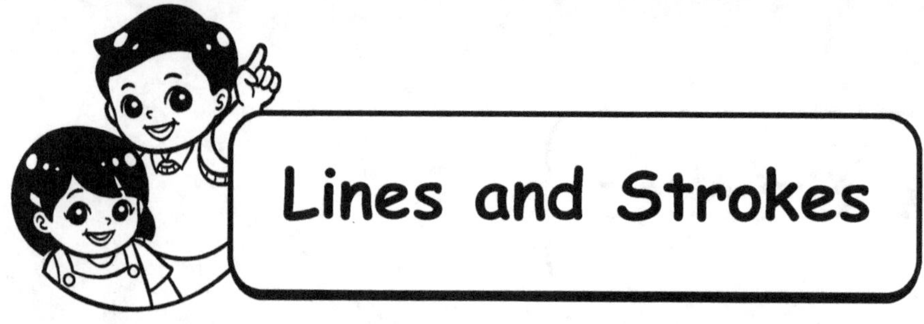

Lines and Strokes

Straight and Curved Lines

Trace the lines on the iguana. Color the picture after.

Skills: Tracing; Coloring

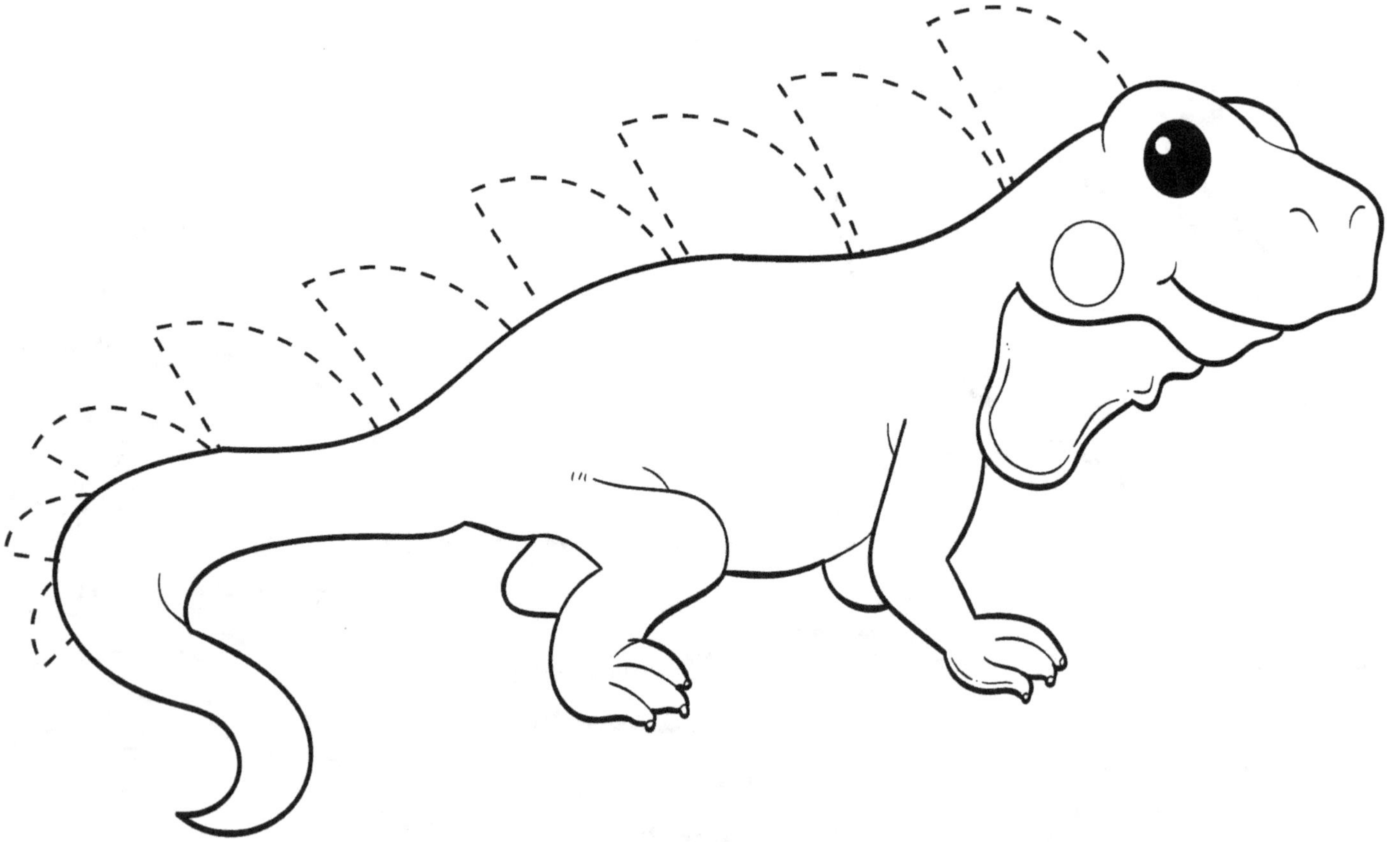

Lines and Strokes

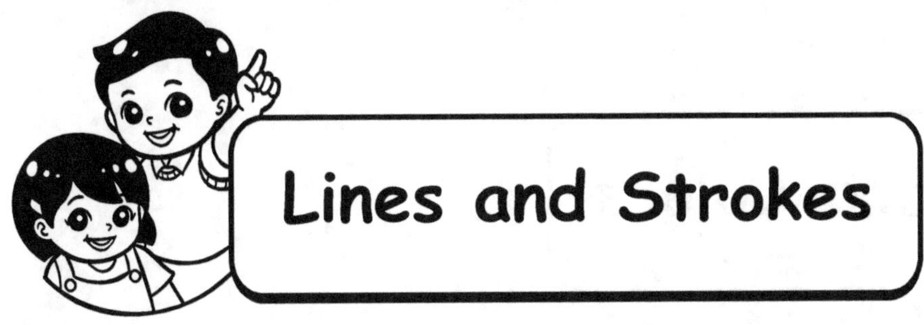

Straight and Curved Lines

Draw some cracks using straight and curved lines on the egg. Paint the egg yellow after.

Skills: Drawing; Painting

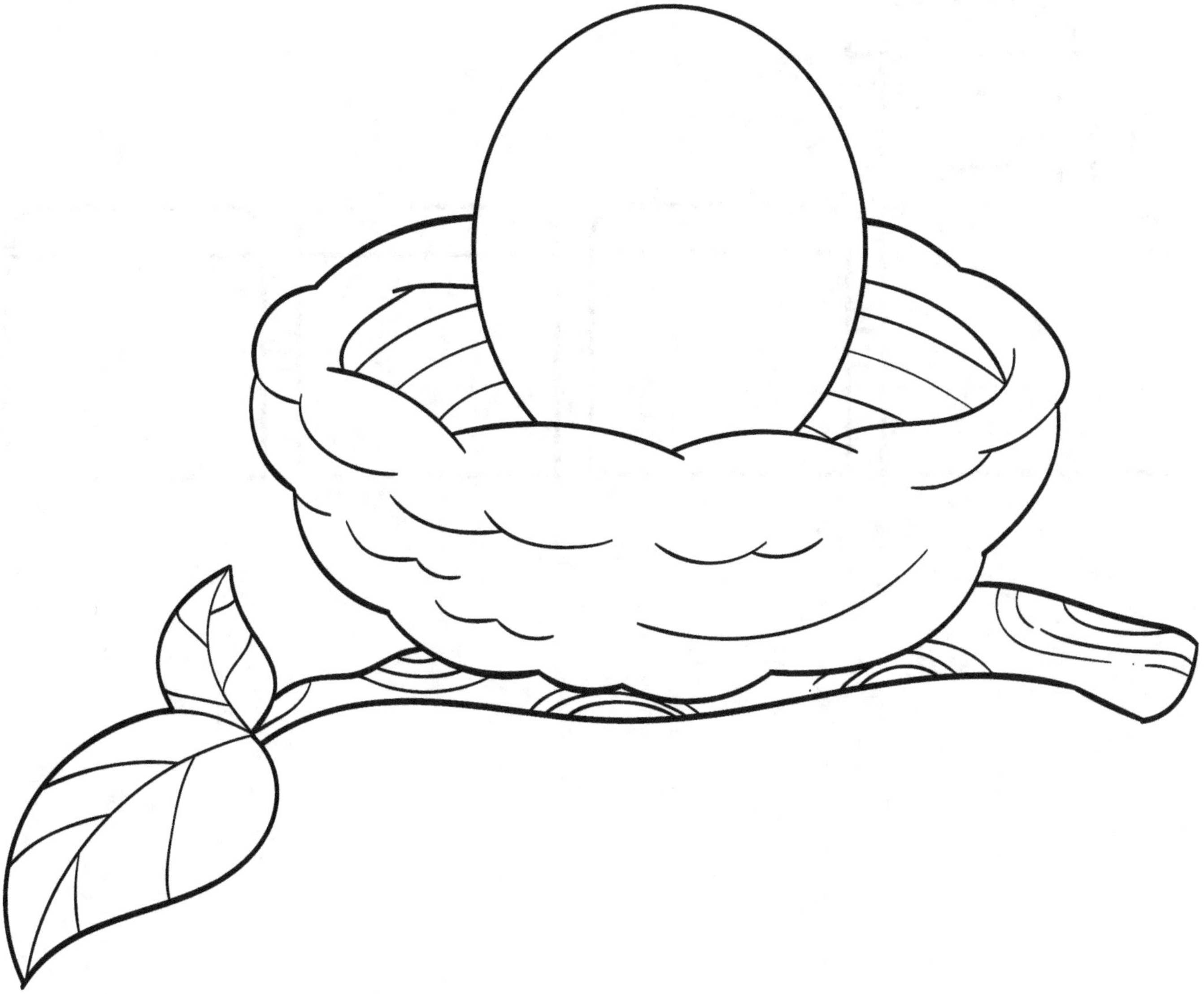

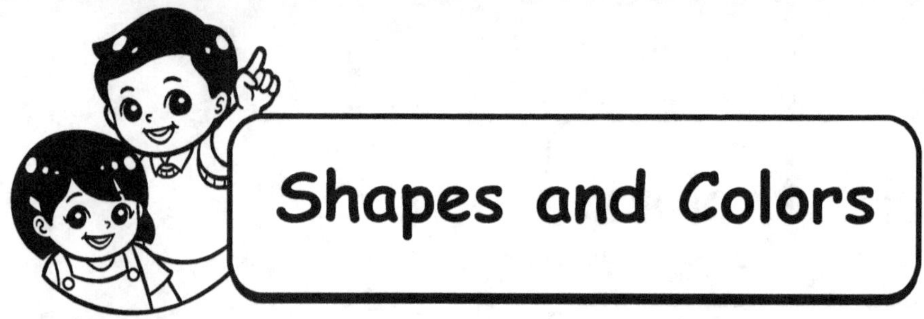

Circle

Cut and paste circles from colored paper to make train wheels.

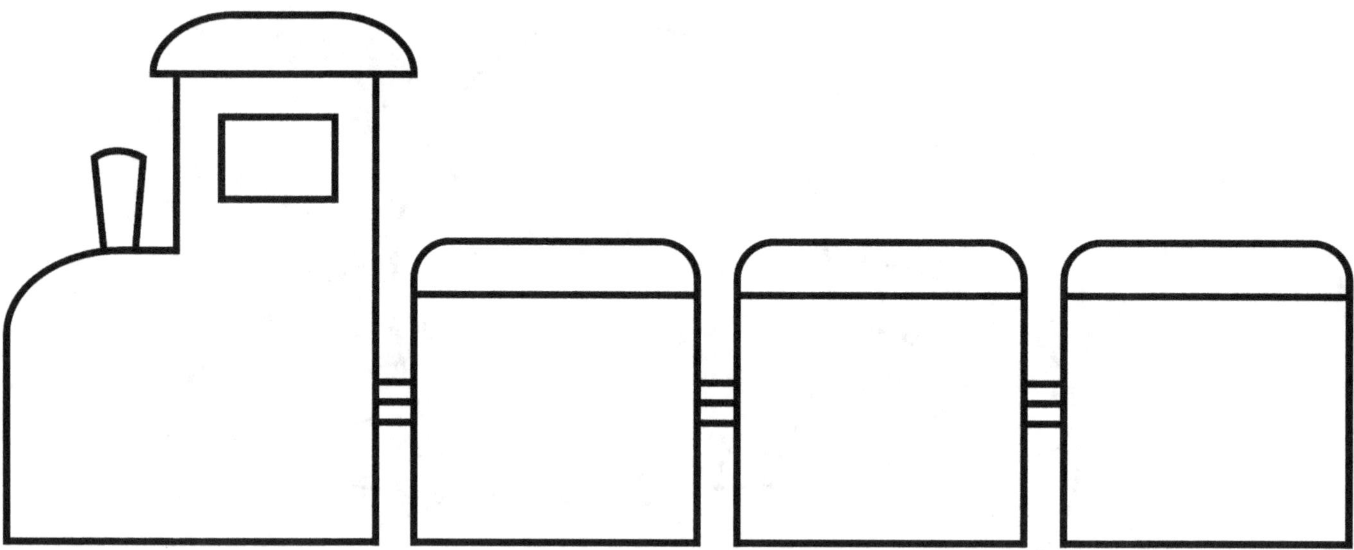

Skills: Cutting; Pasting

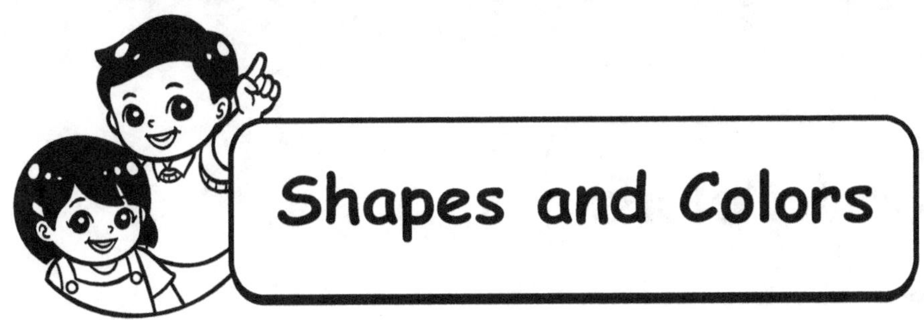

Shapes and Colors

Circle
Color the chocolates.

Shapes and Colors

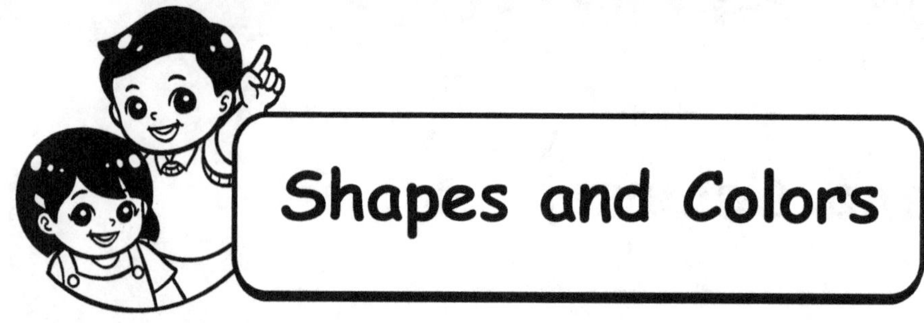

Triangle

Draw triangles to make the sail. Color the picture after.

Skills: Drawing; Coloring

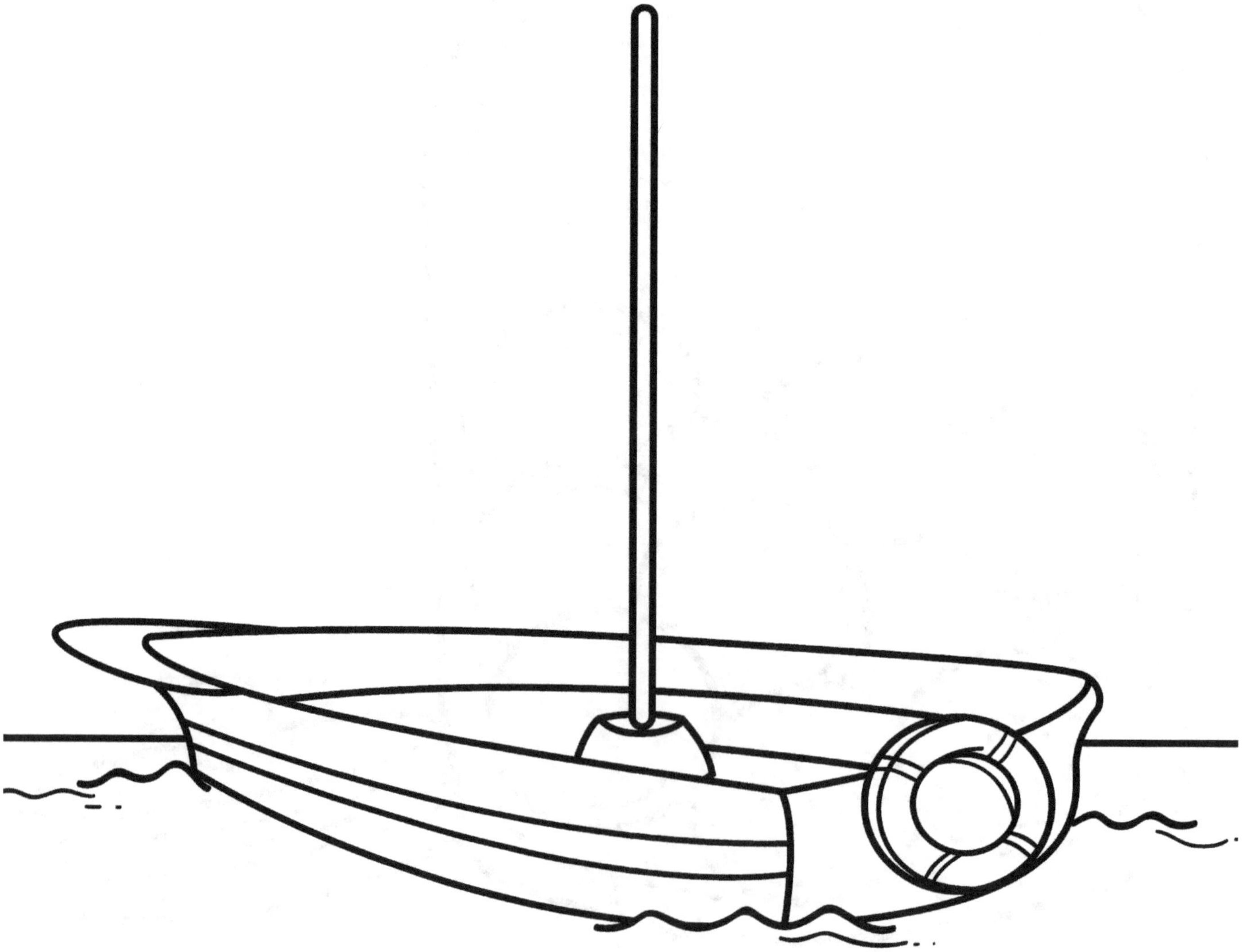

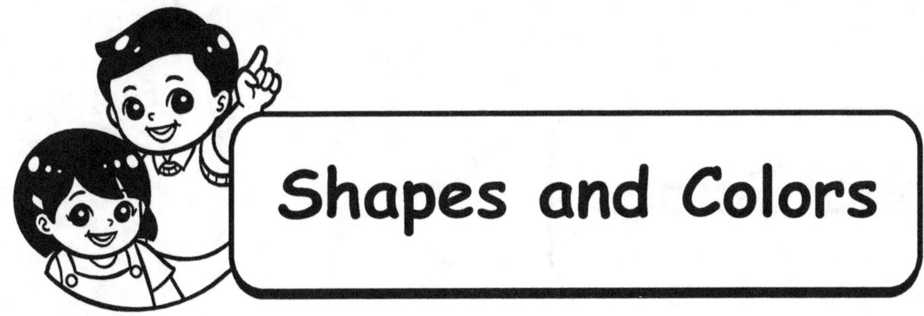

Triangle

Cut and paste three triangles from colored paper to make fins and a tail. Color the picture after.

Shapes and Colors

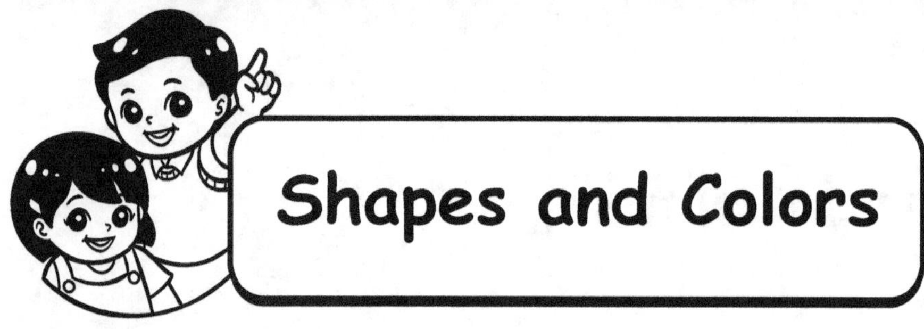

Square

Connect the dots to make gift boxes.

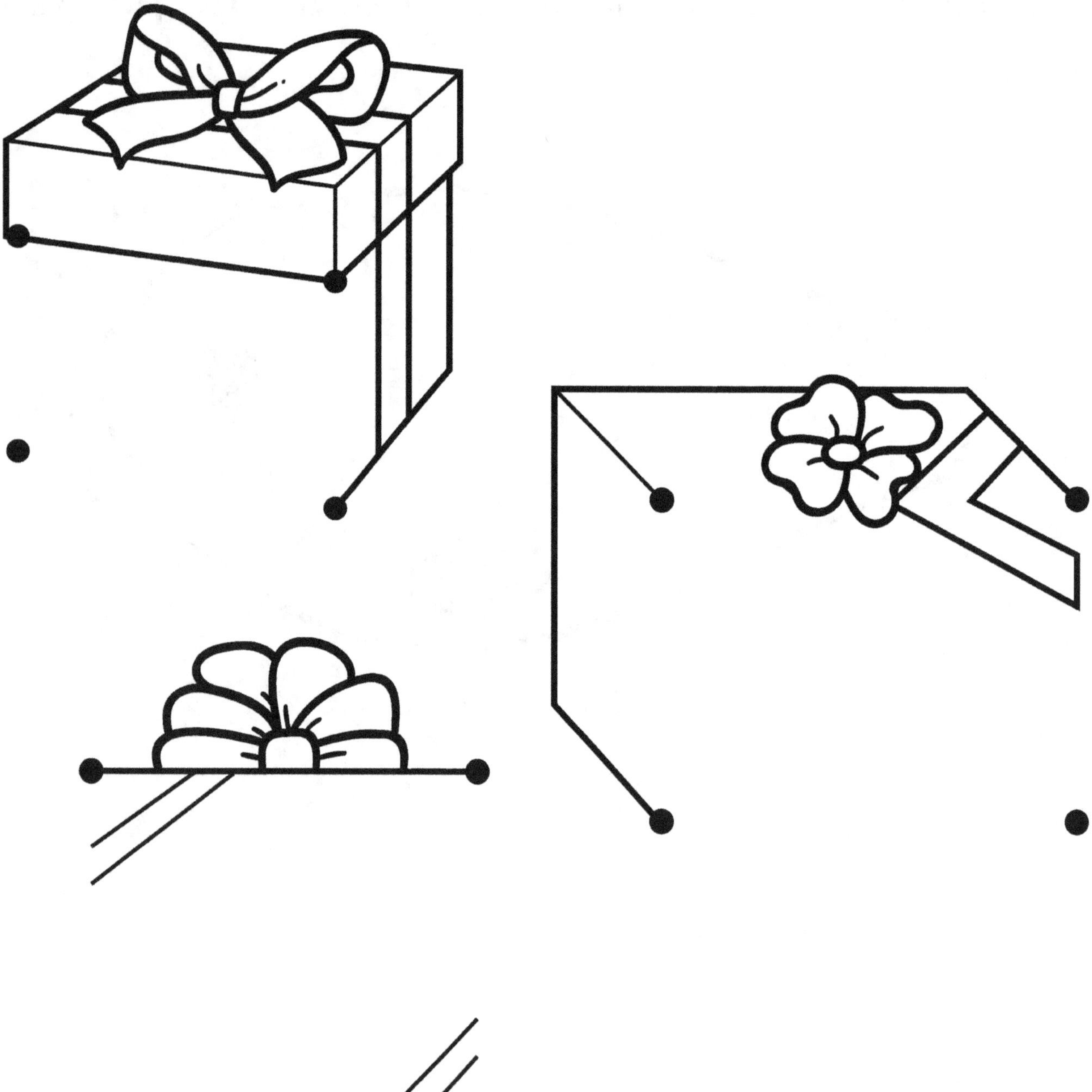

Shapes and Colors

Square

Paste sticks to make borders.

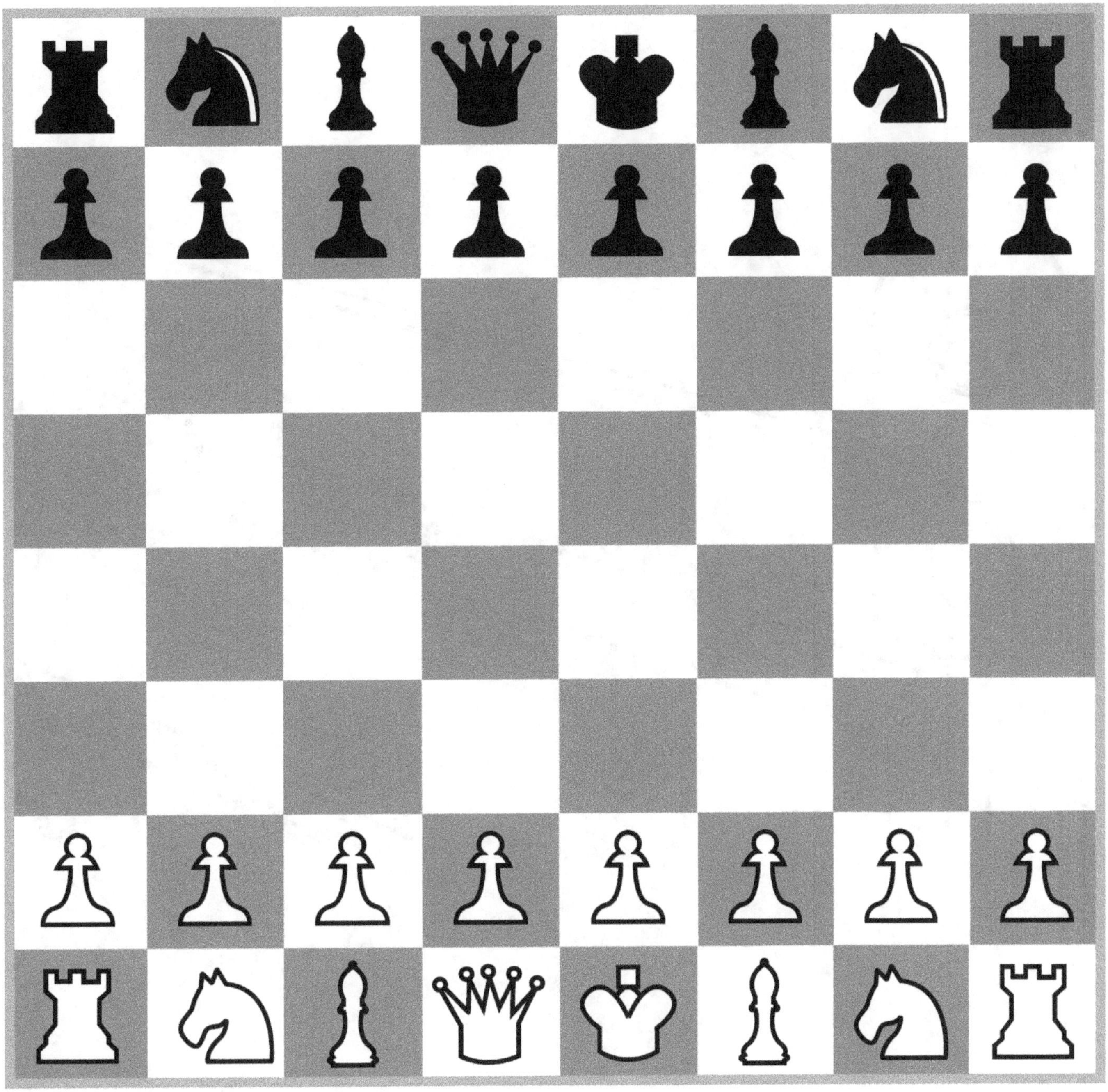

Shapes and Colors

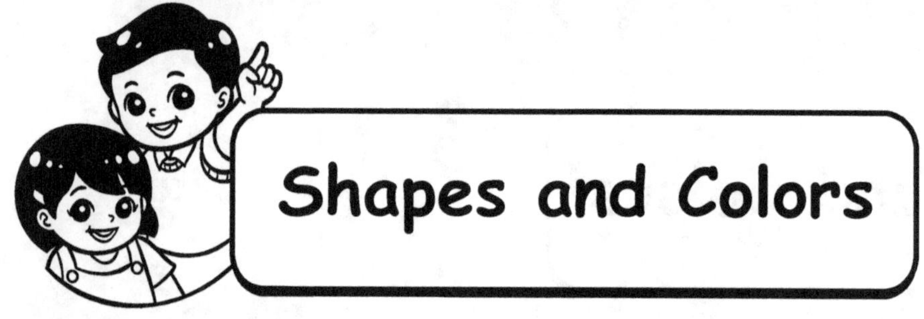

Rectangle

Connect the dots and color the rectangles.

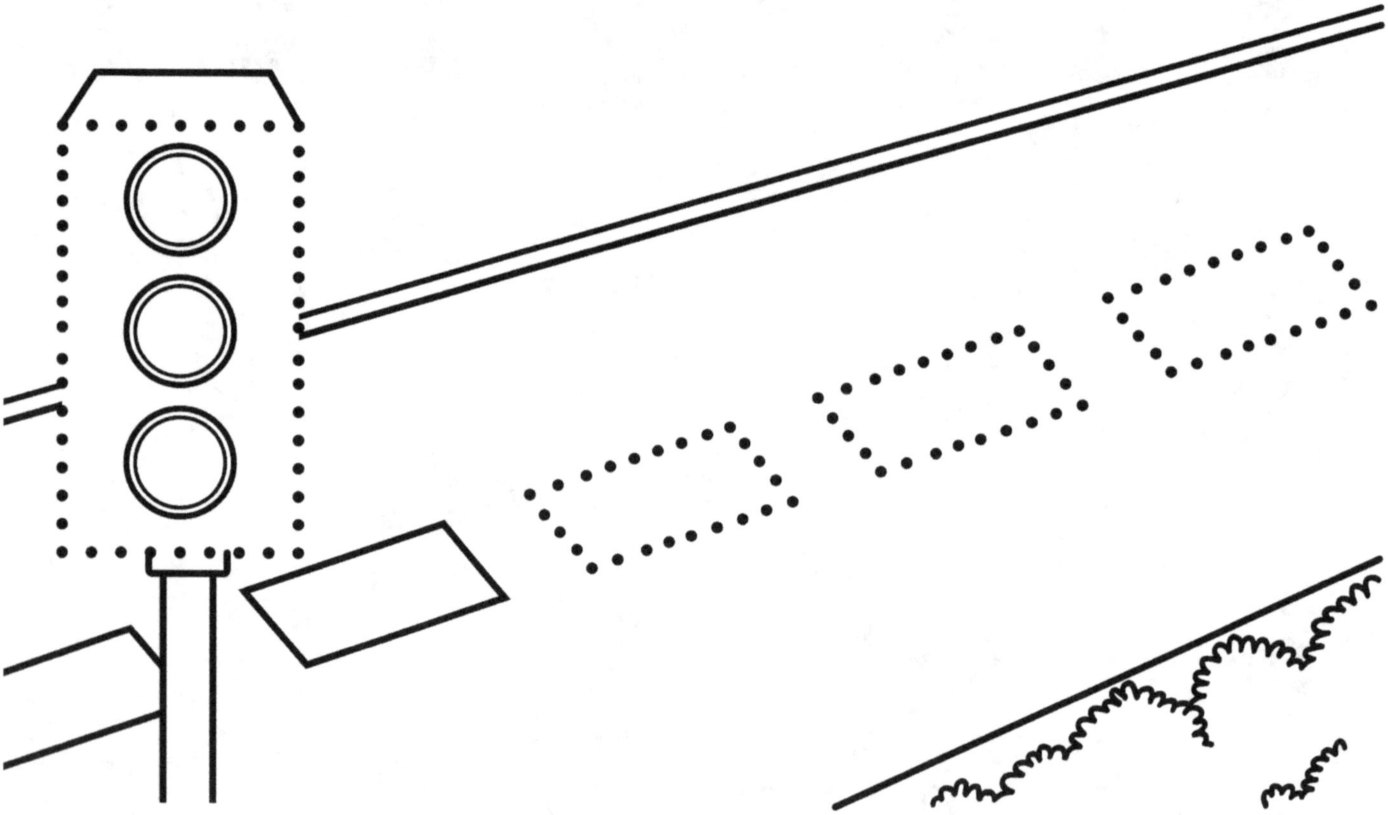

Skills: Prewriting; Coloring; Tracing

Shapes and Colors

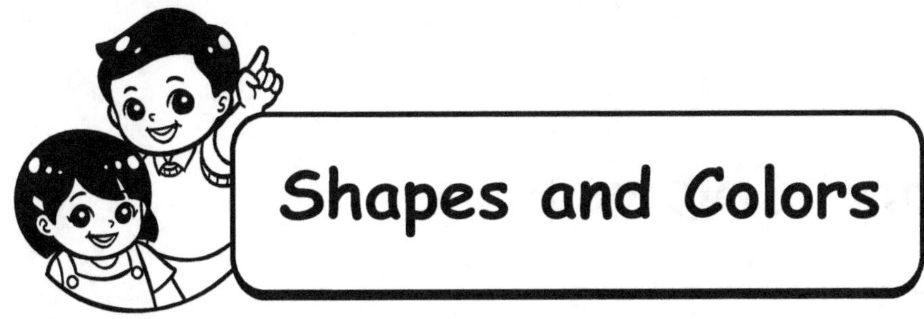

Rectangle

Stamp red paint with your thumb on the body of the fire truck.

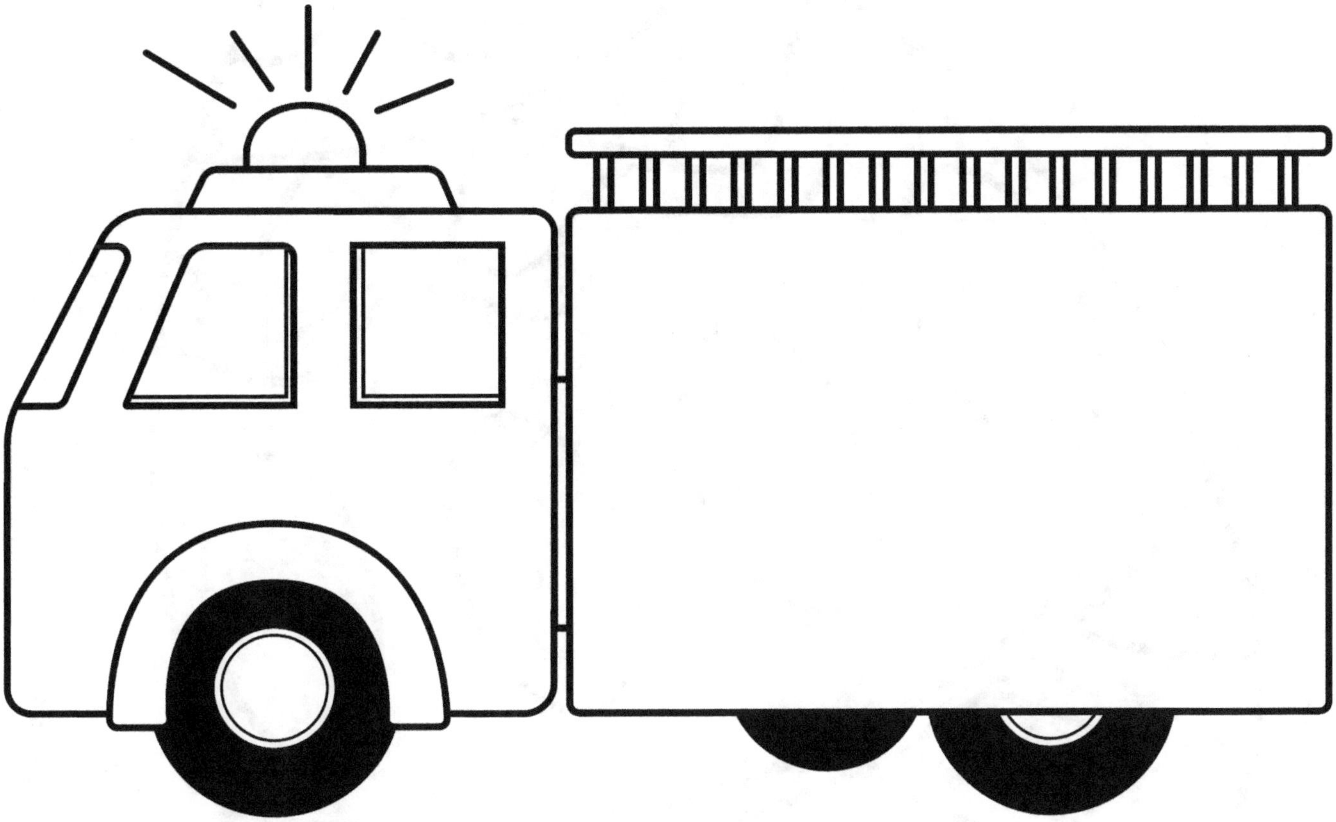

Oblong

Color the Easter egg.

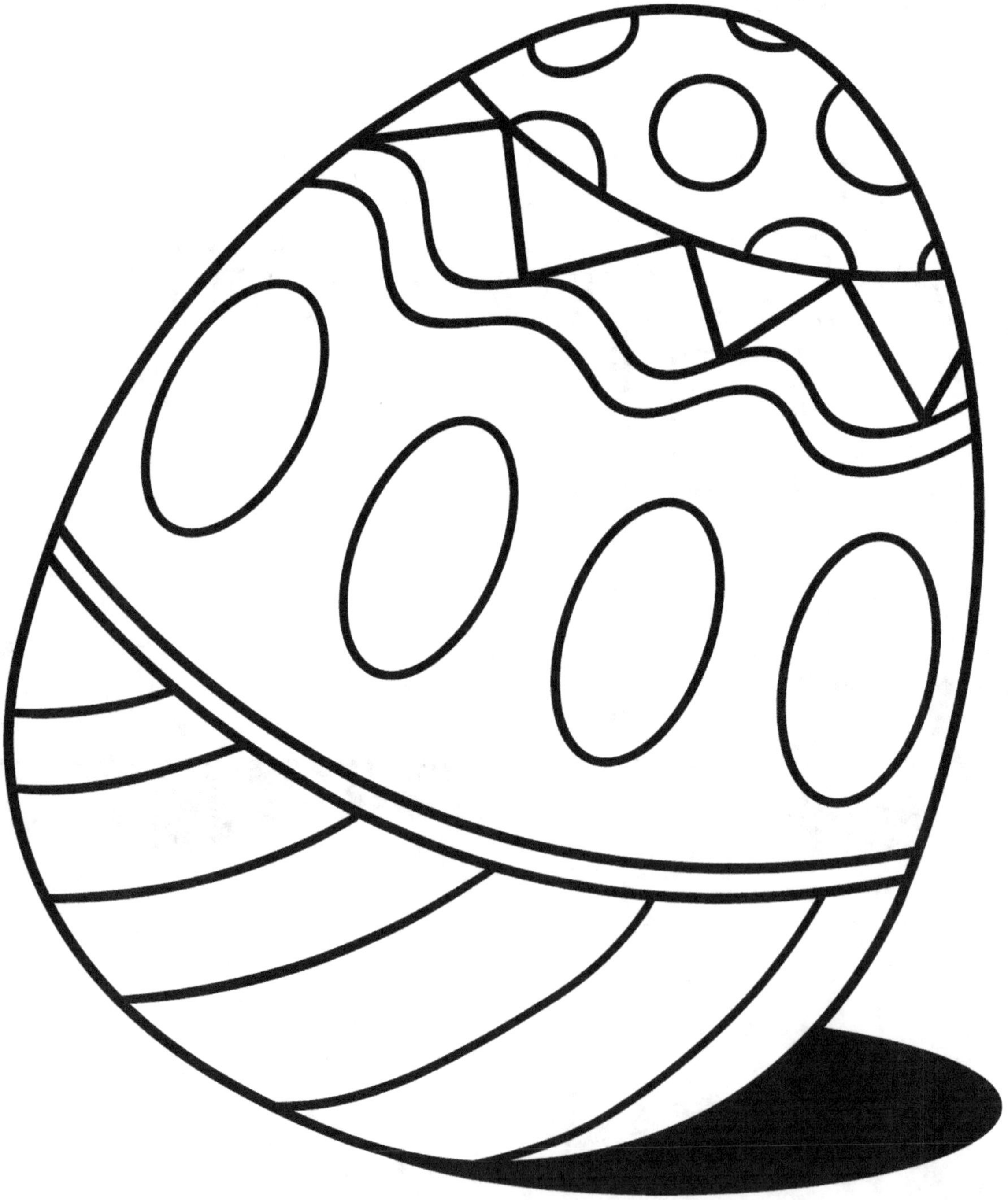

Skills: Coloring

Shapes and Colors

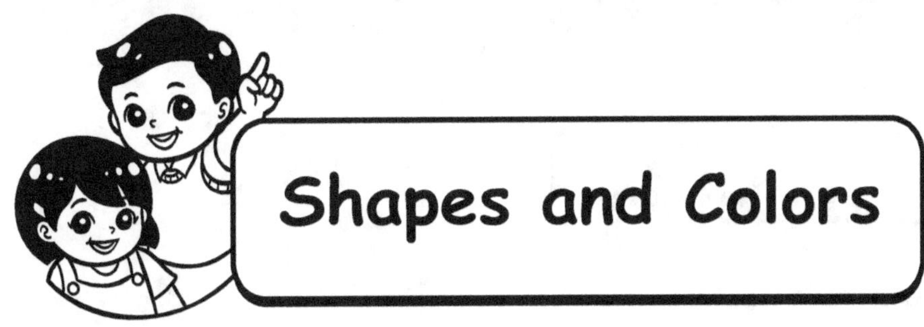

Oblong

Cut out oblongs from a white sheet of paper. Paste oblongs on the tray to make eggs.

Skills: Pasting; Cutting

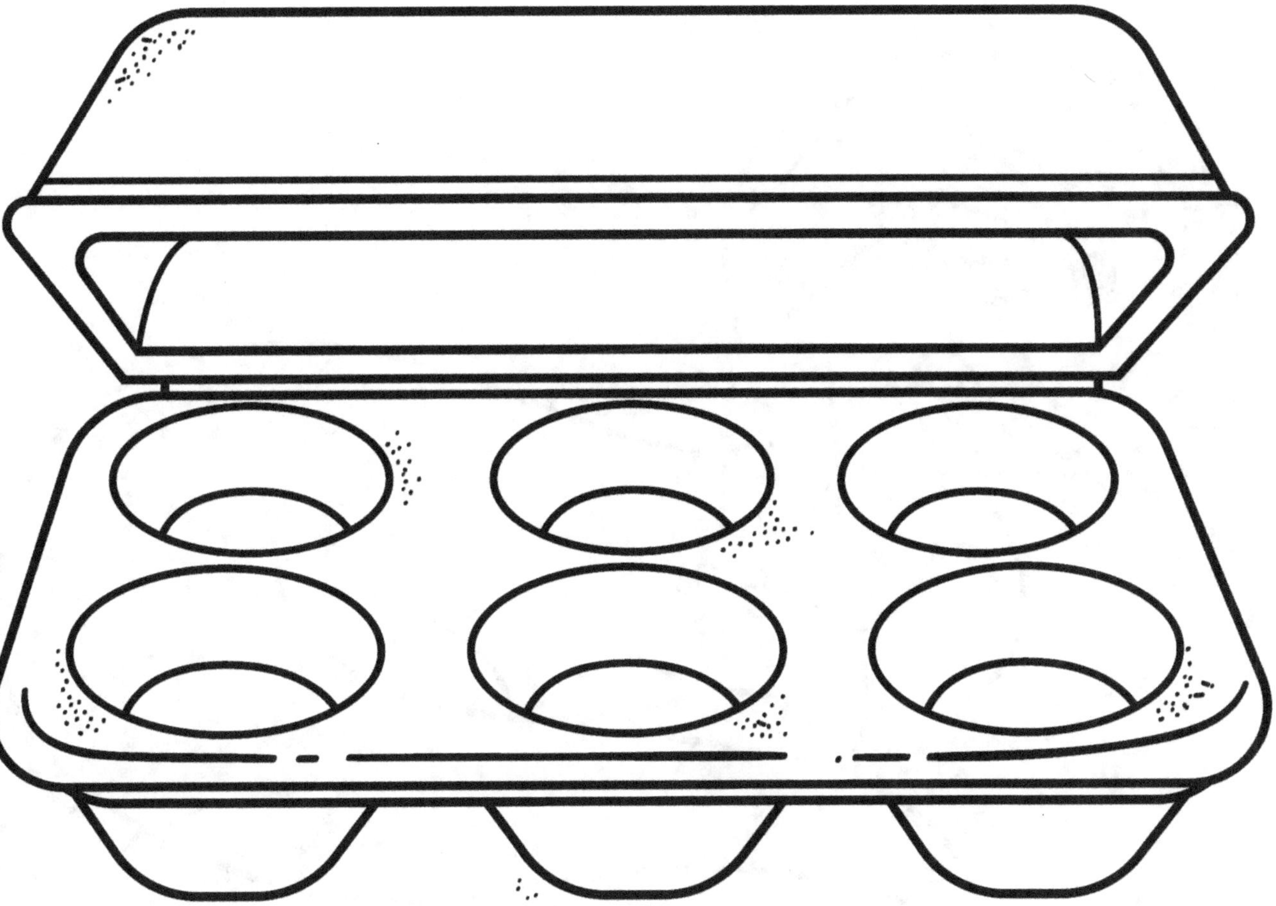

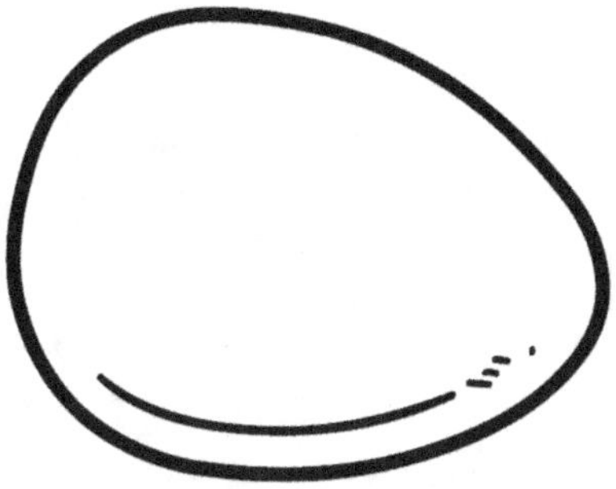

Shapes and Colors

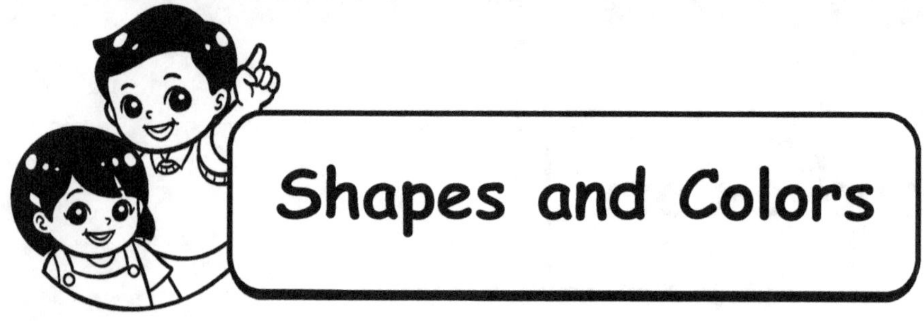

Diamond

Cut out diamond shapes from colored paper. Paste the diamonds on the body of the dragon.

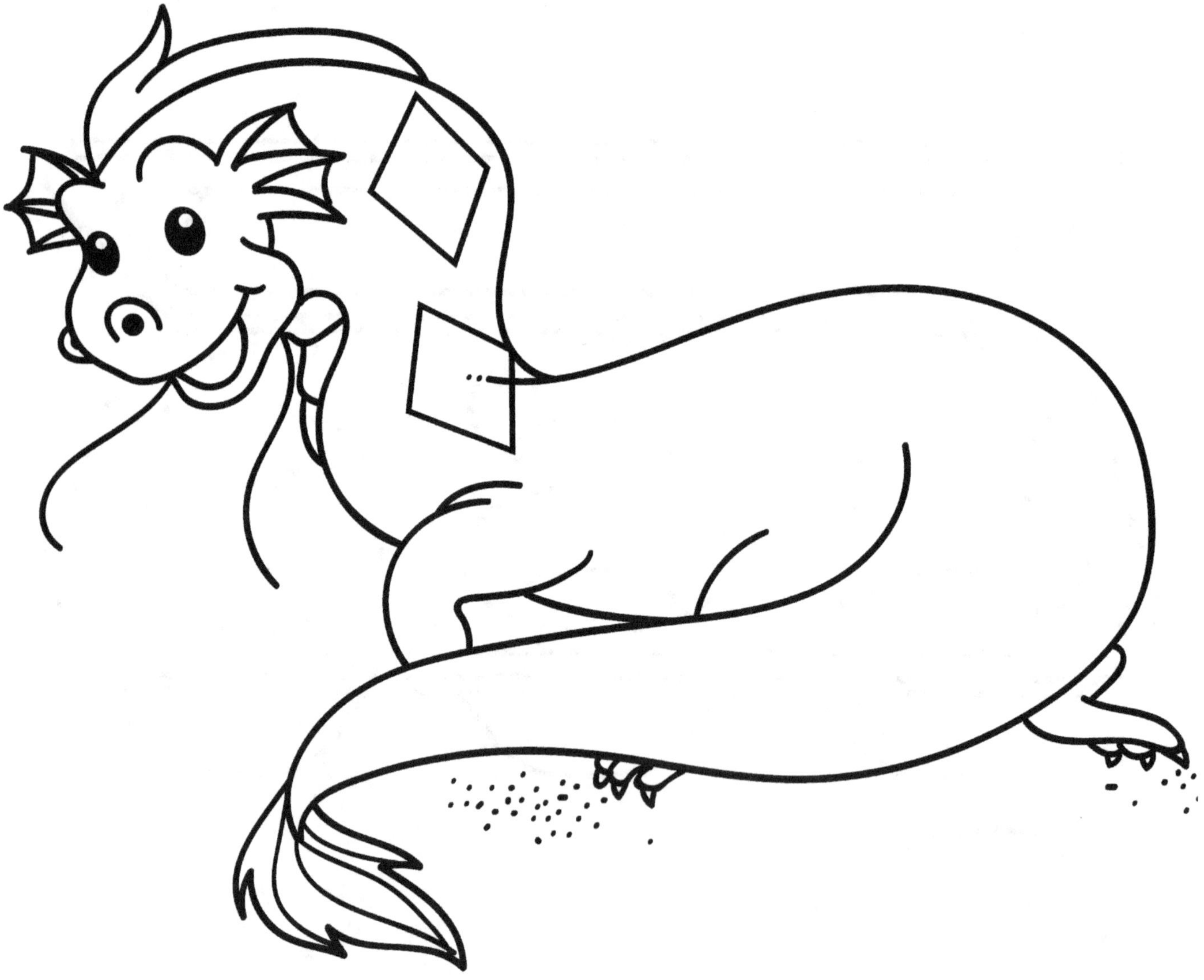

Skills: Pasting; Cutting

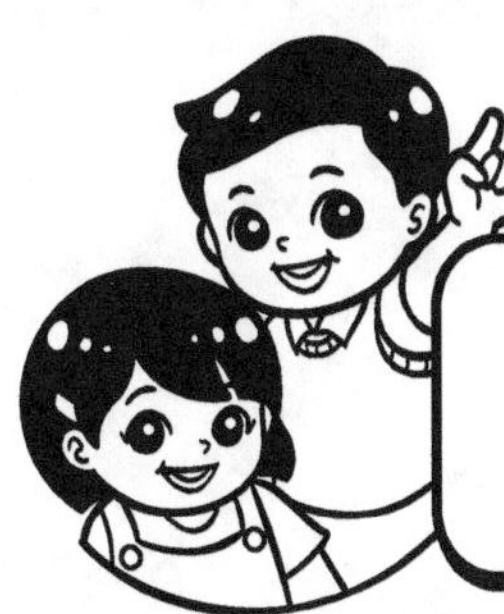

Diamond

Paste four toothpicks to make the fox's diamond tail.

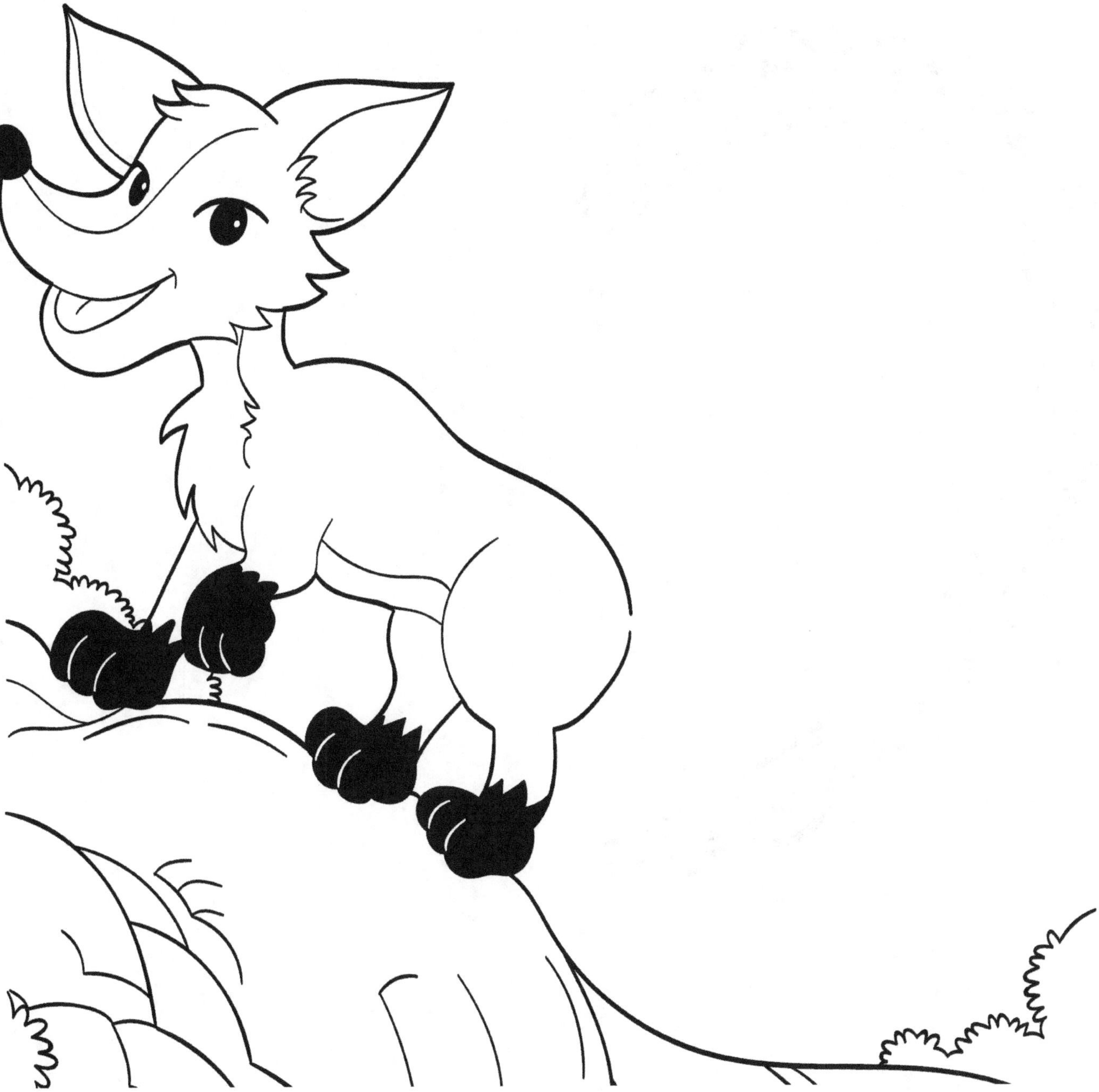

Skills: Pasting; Counting

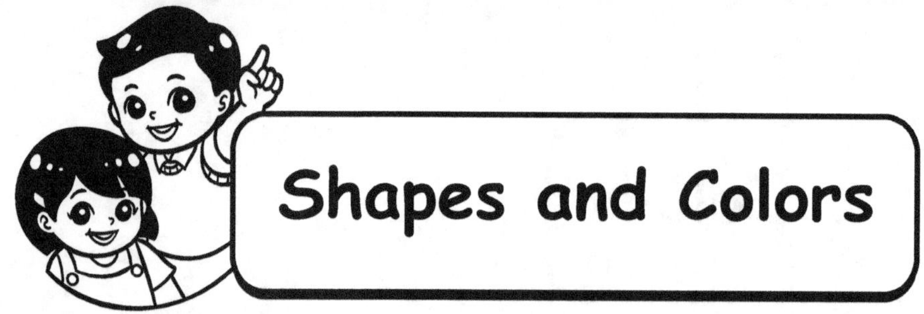

Heart

Complete the laced heart. Color it after.

Skills: Symmetrical Thinking; Drawing; Coloring

Shapes and Colors

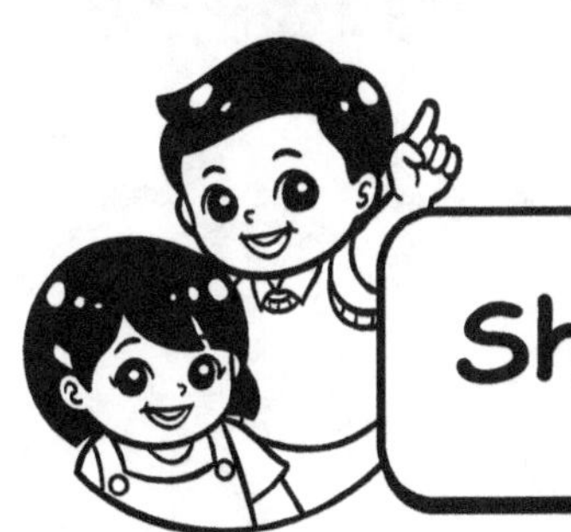

Heart

Draw a heart inside the hands. Color it after.

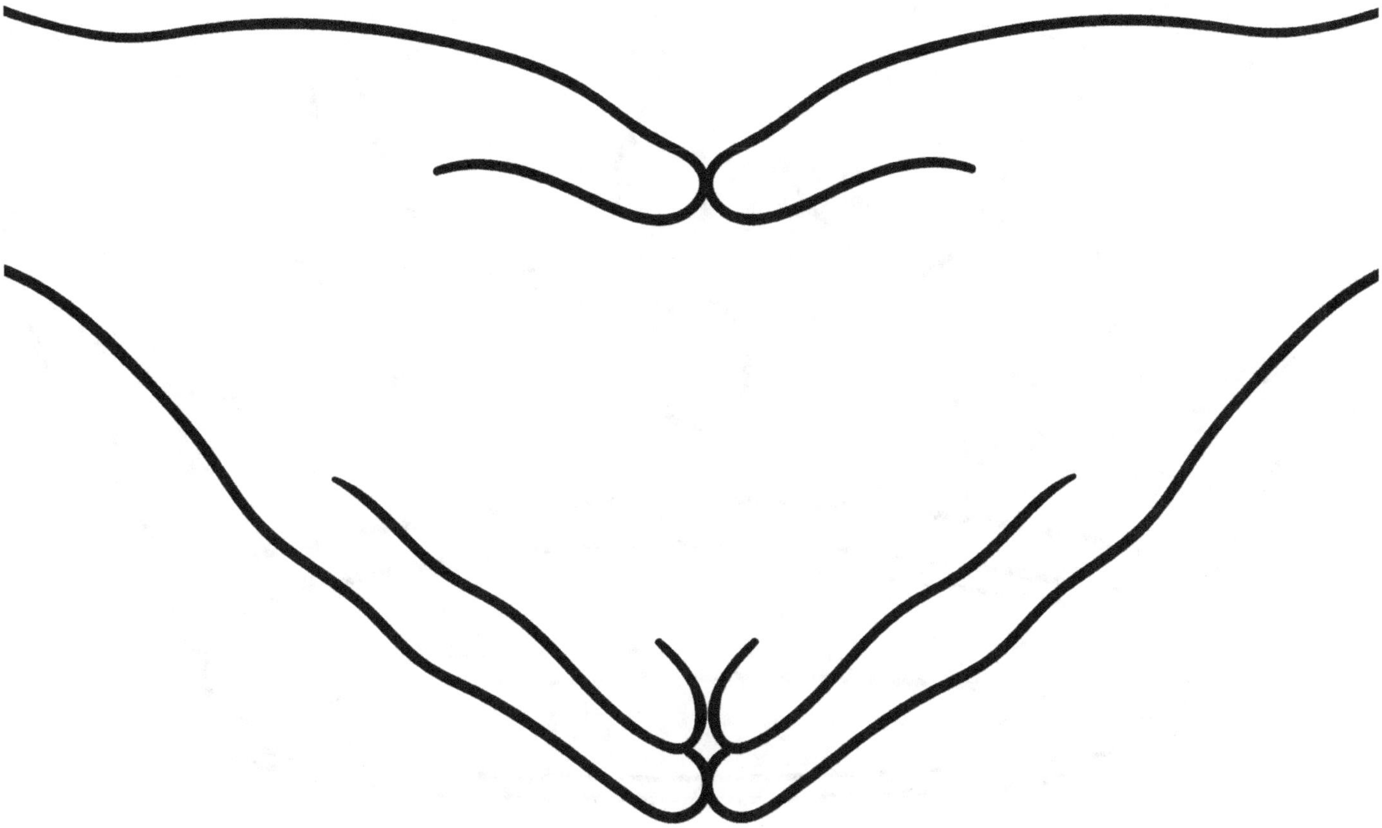

Skills: Drawing; Coloring

Shapes and Colors

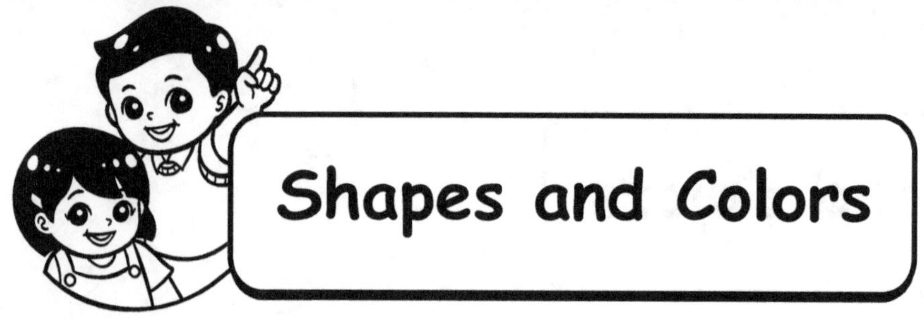

Star

Draw stars on the tips of the crown. Color the picture after.

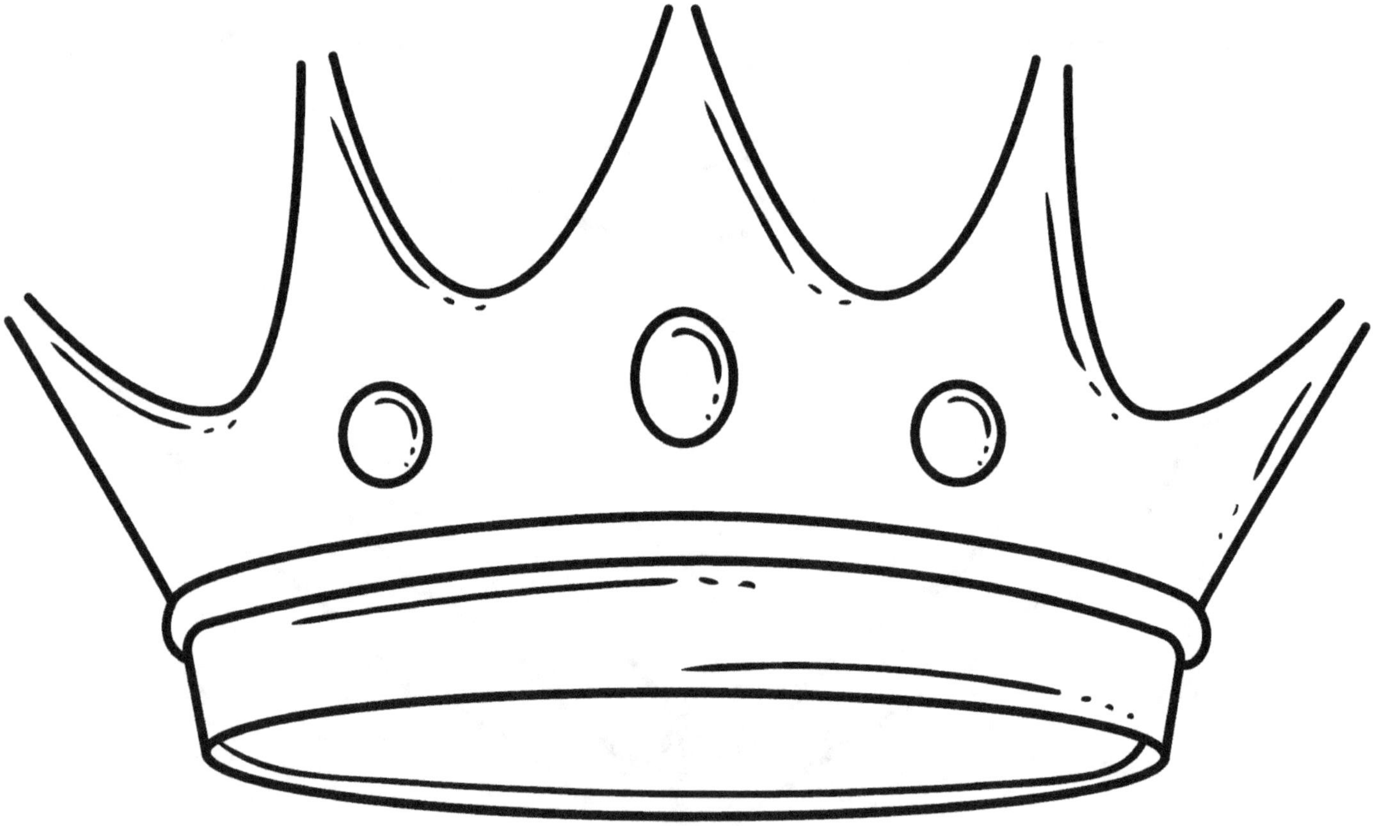

Skills: Drawing; Coloring

Shapes and Colors

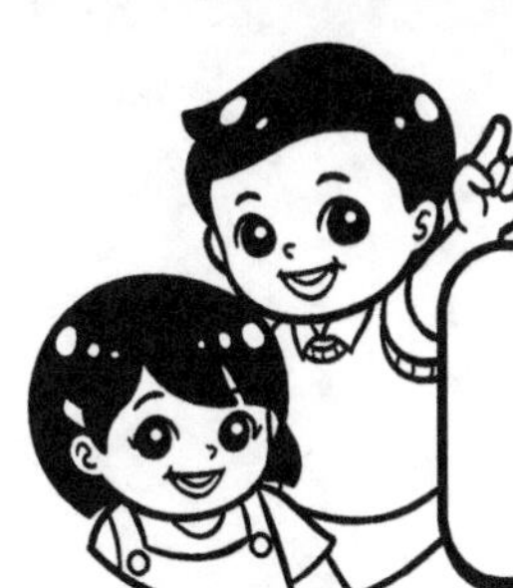

Star

Color the star. Paint it with glue with a bit of water after to make it shiny.

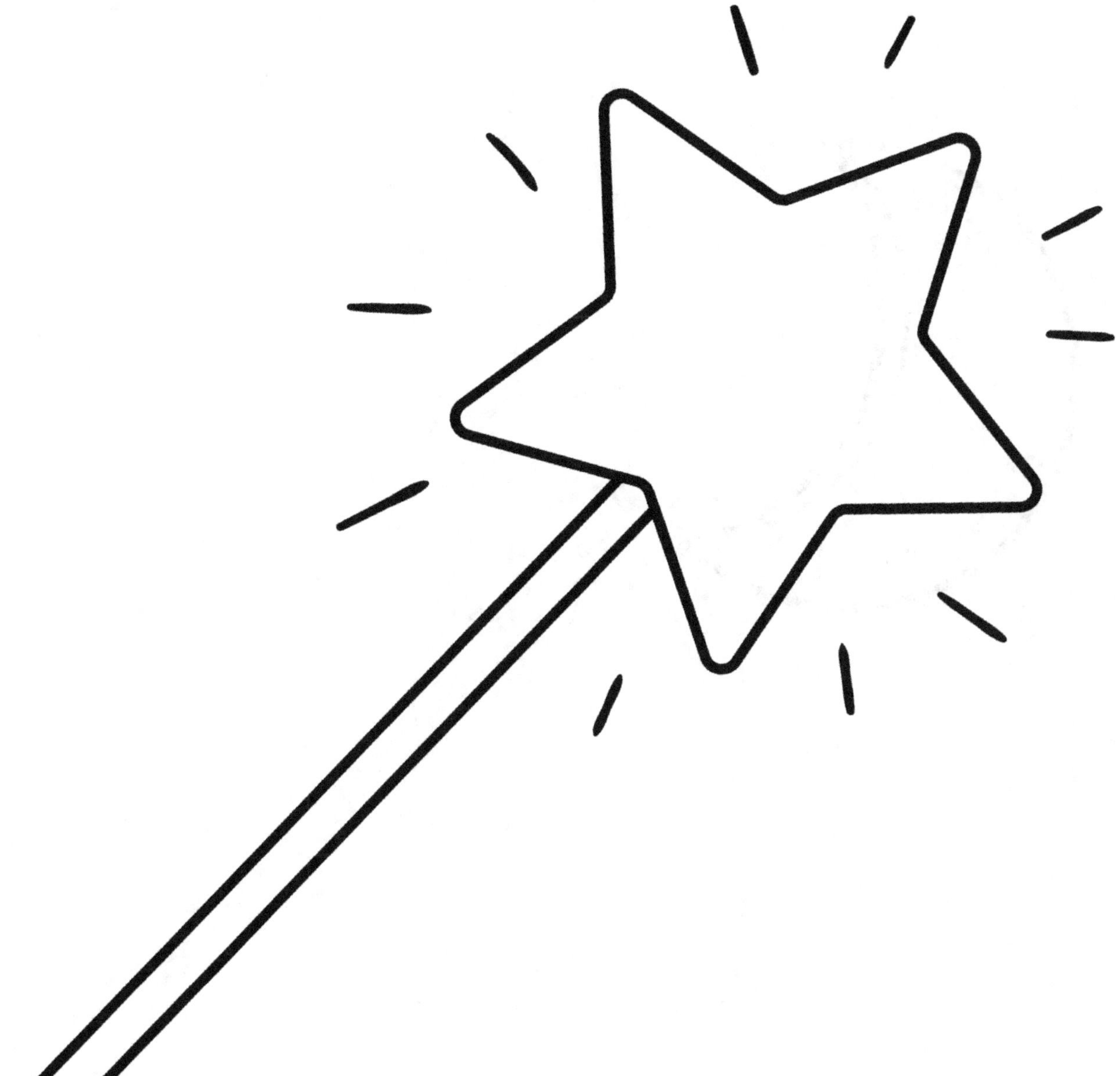

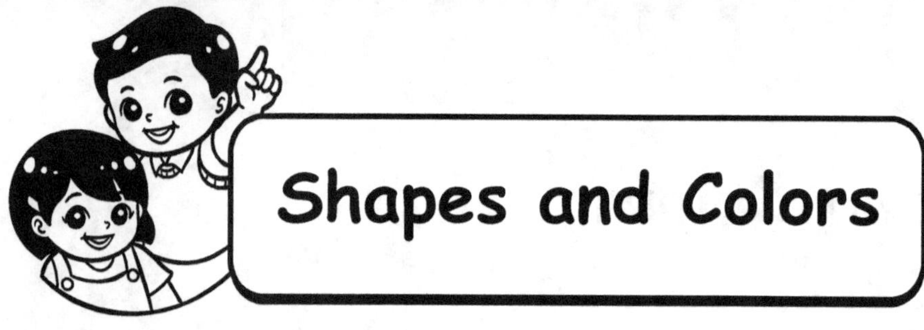

Crescent

Color the moon yellow. Paint the rest of the space black.

Skills: Coloring; Painting

Shapes and Colors

Crescent

Draw crescents to complete the boats. Color the picture after.

Shapes and Colors

Draw a moon and a star among the clouds.   Draw a rocket ship using triangles △, rectangles ☐, and circles ◯.

Shapes and Colors

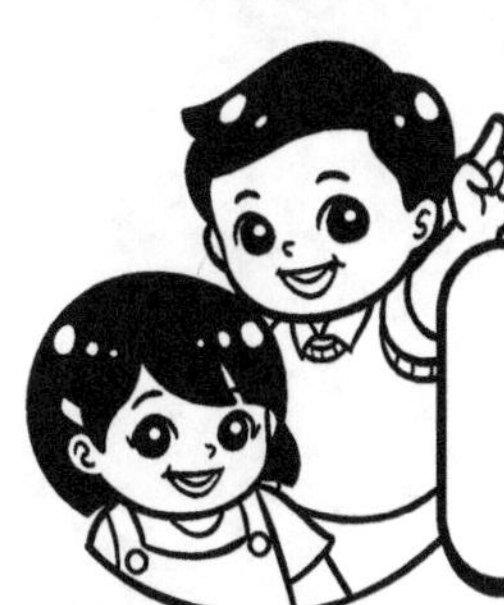

Color the shapes. Cut out the stick and shapes then paste them together to make a shape barbecue.

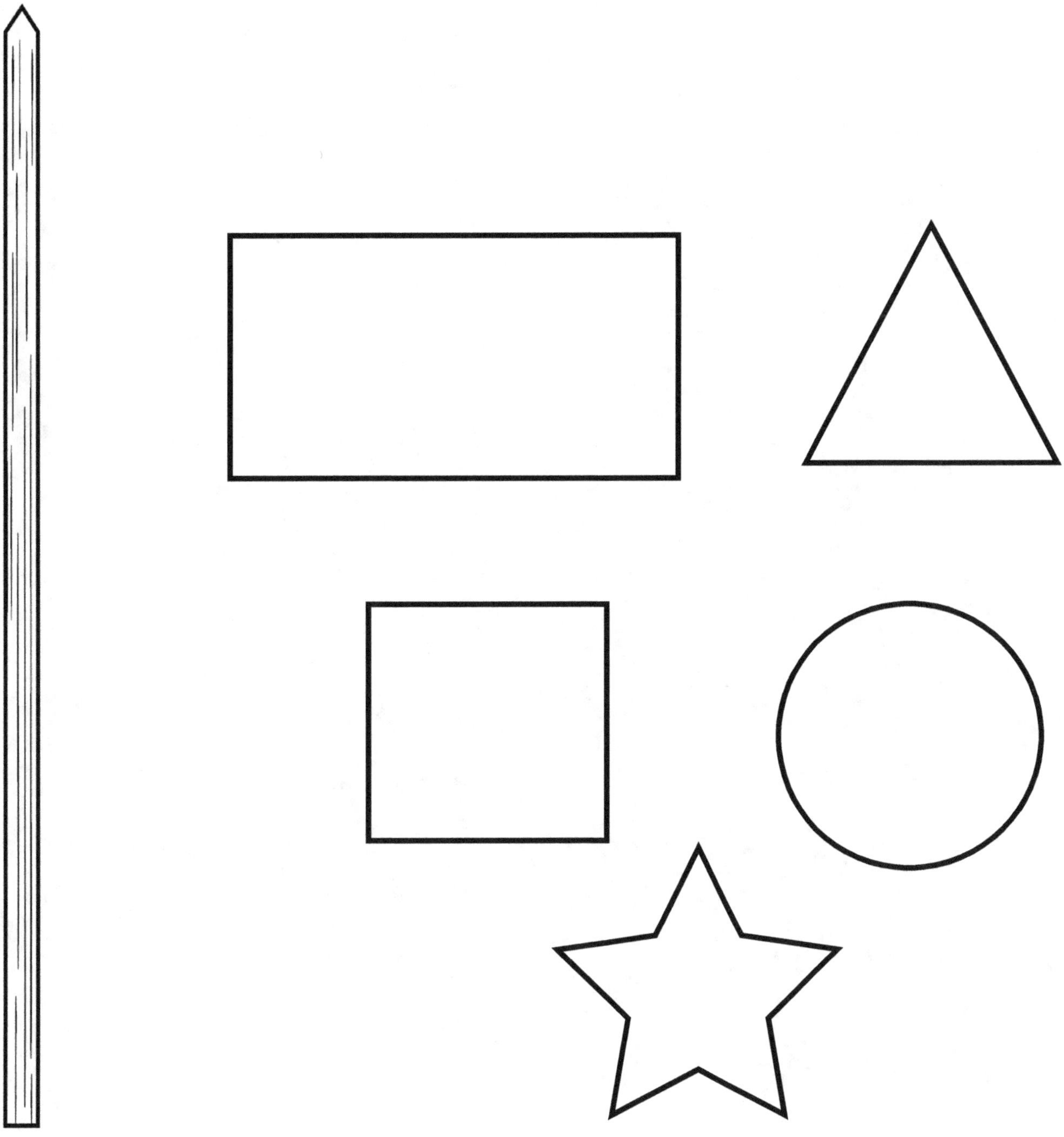

Skills: Coloring; Cutting; Pasting

Red

Color the bug red.

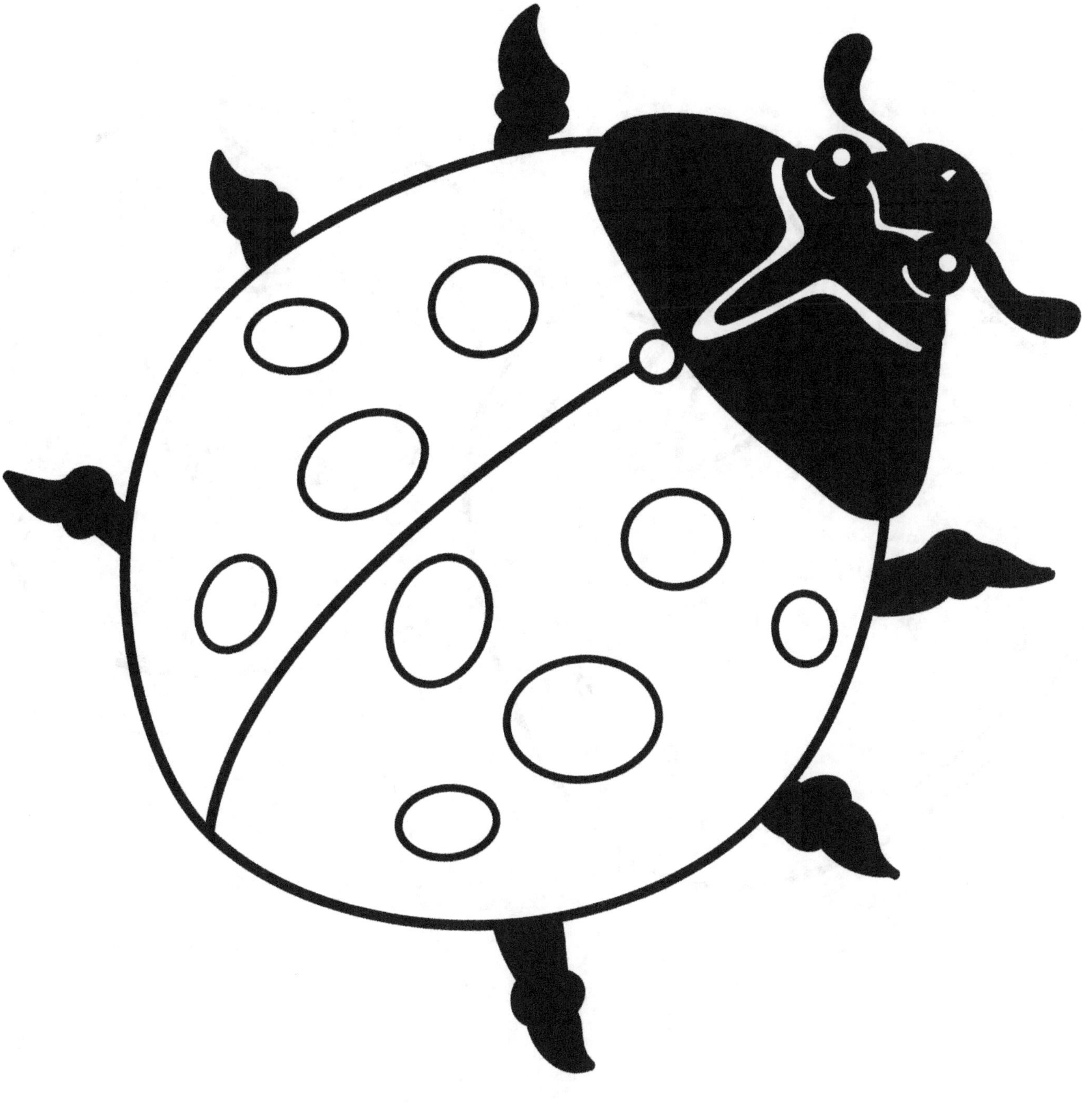

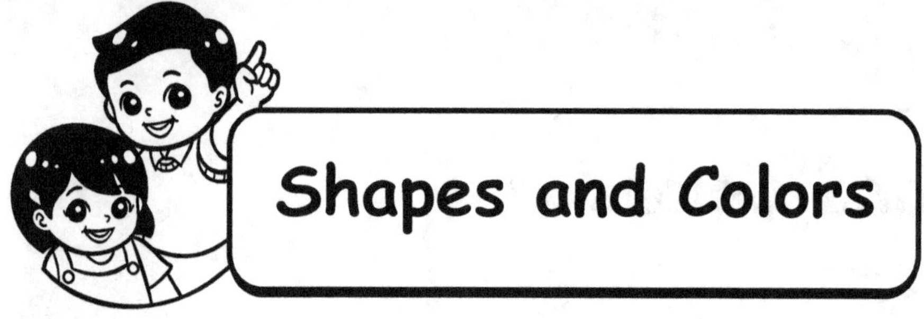

Shapes and Colors

Red

Paint the strawberries red. Sprinkle some salt after.

Skills: Painting; Fine Motor

Shapes and Colors

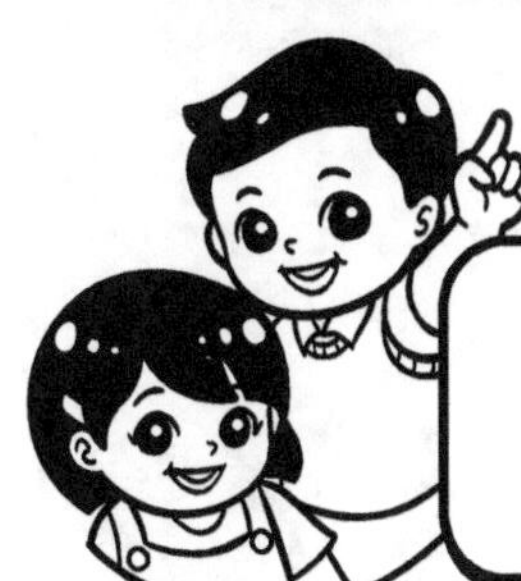

Yellow

Color the fireflies yellow.

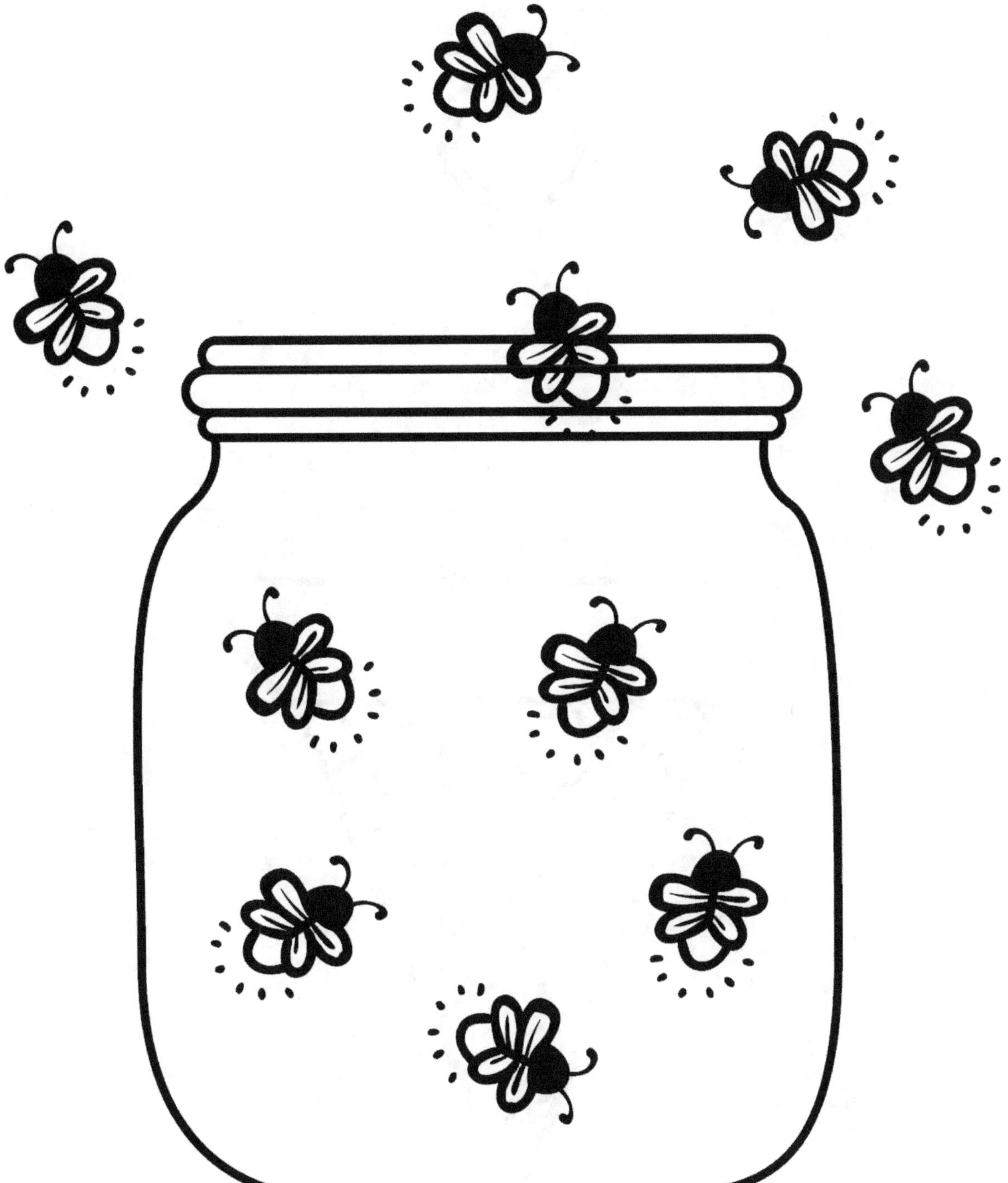

Yellow

Tear yellow paper. Paste them to make ice cream.

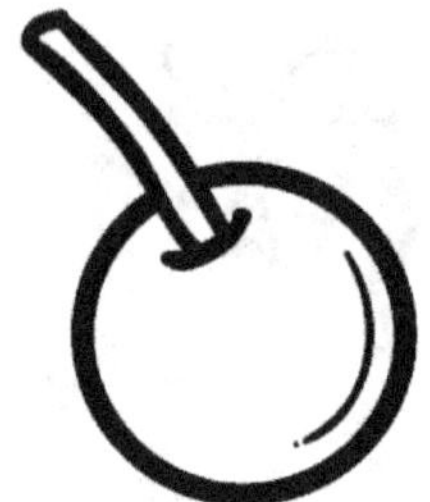

Skills: Paper Tearing; Pasting

Shapes and Colors

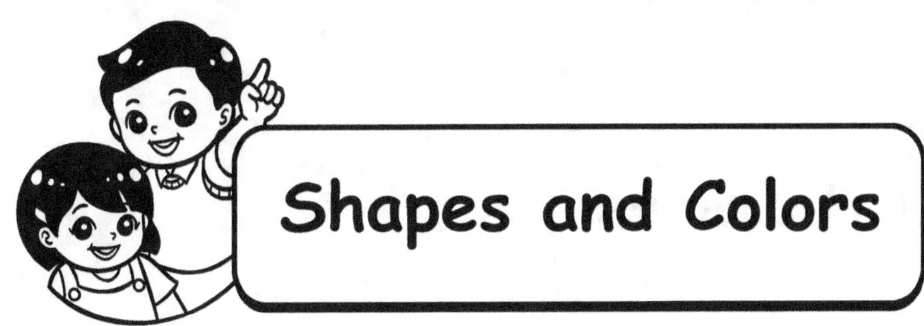

Blue

Color the peacock blue.

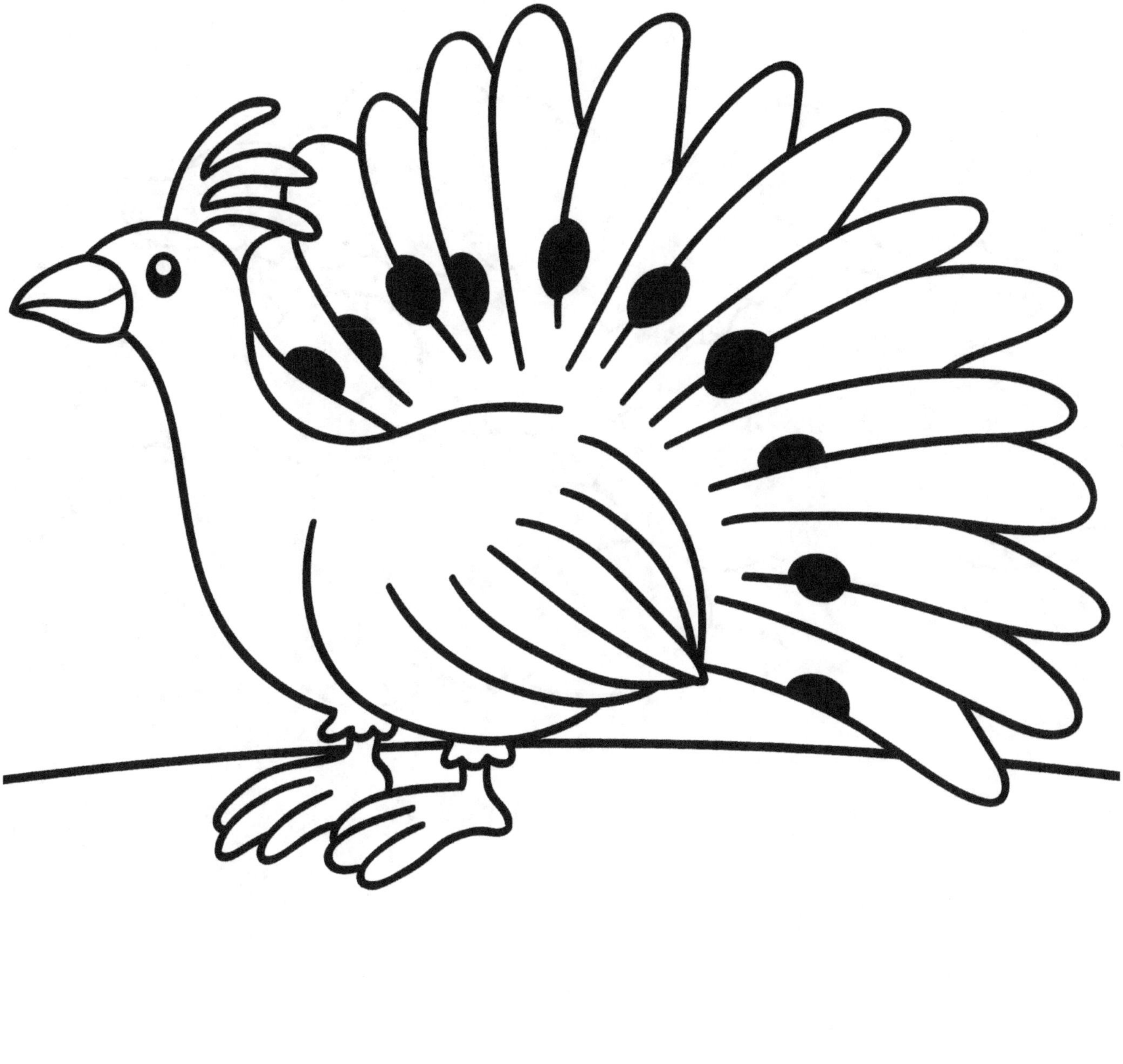

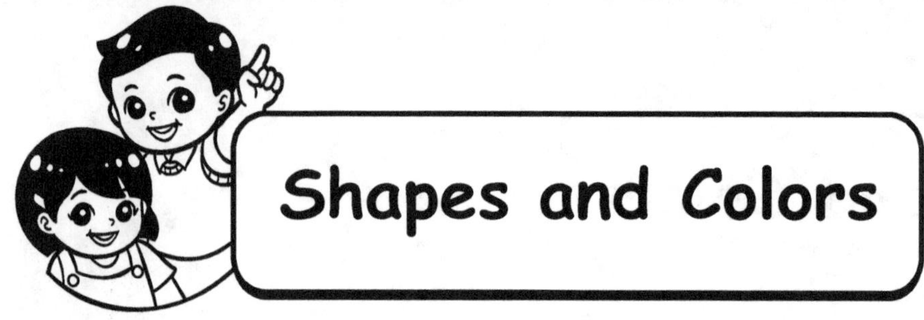

Shapes and Colors

Blue

Paste cotton on the clouds. Drip blue paint after.

Skills: Pasting; Fine Motor

Shapes and Colors

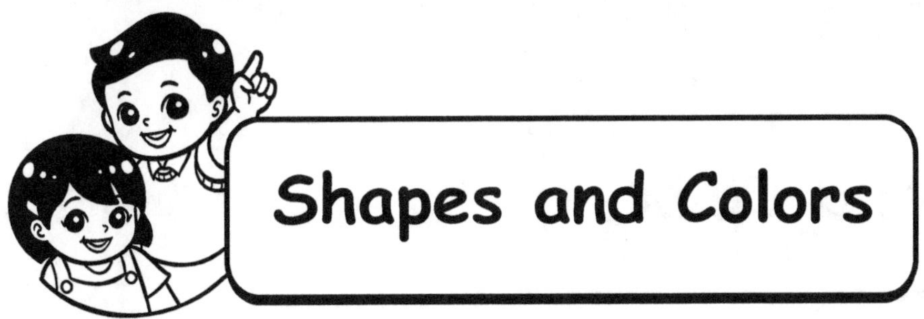

Green

Paste green circles on the caterpillar.

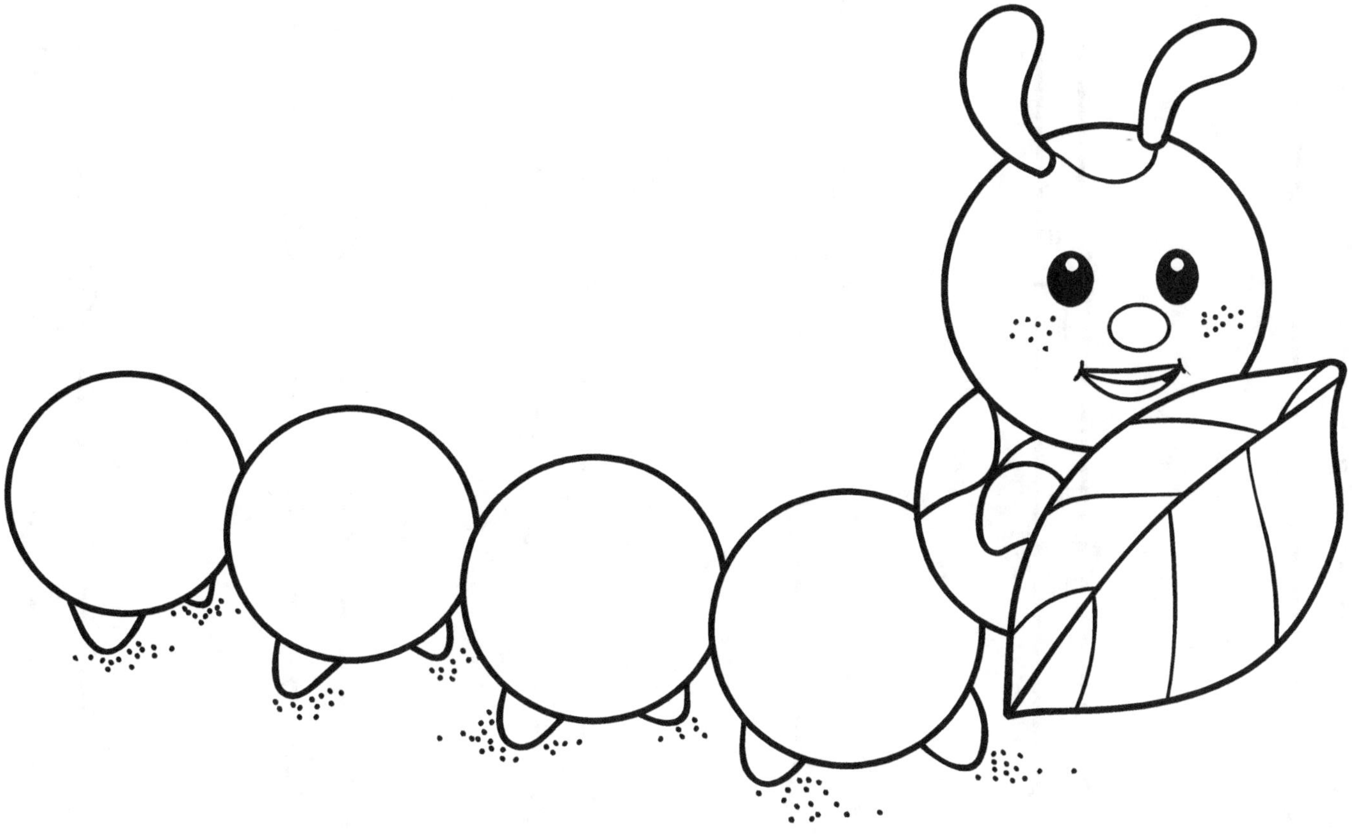

Shapes and Colors

Green

Dip your thumb on green paint. Stamp it to make bamboo leaves.

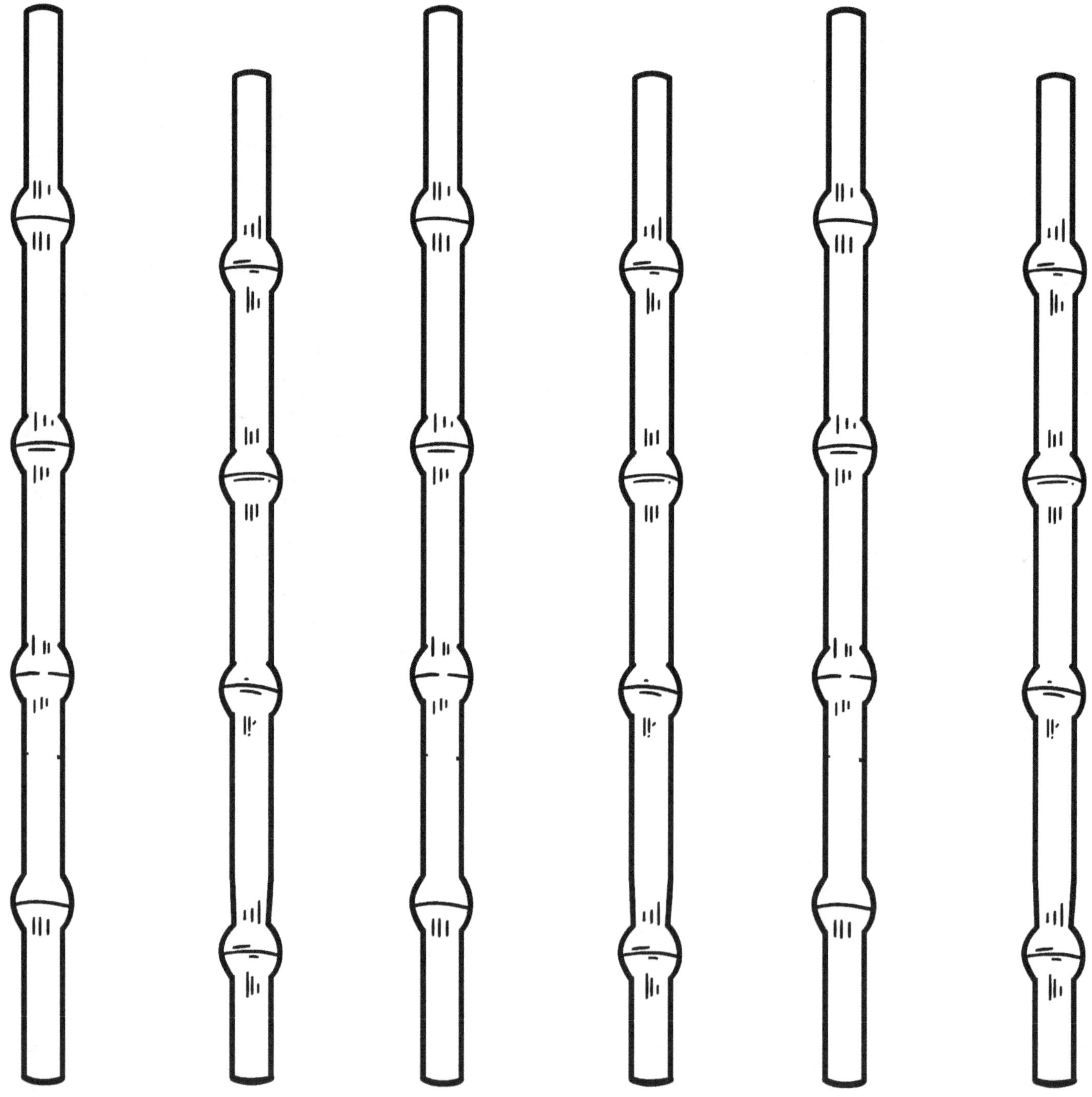

Skills: Stamping

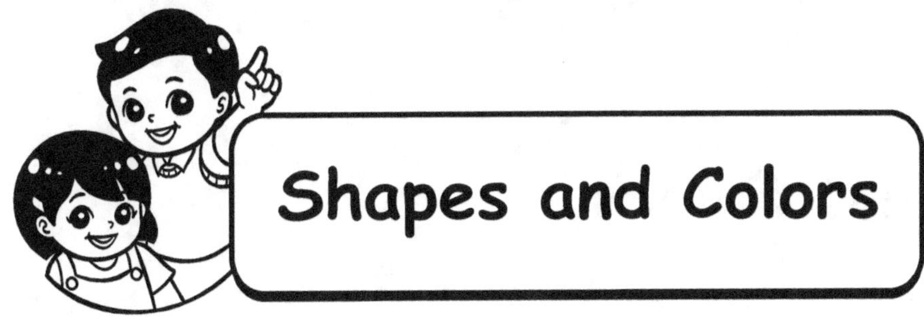

Orange

Finish drawing the ball. Color with orange after.

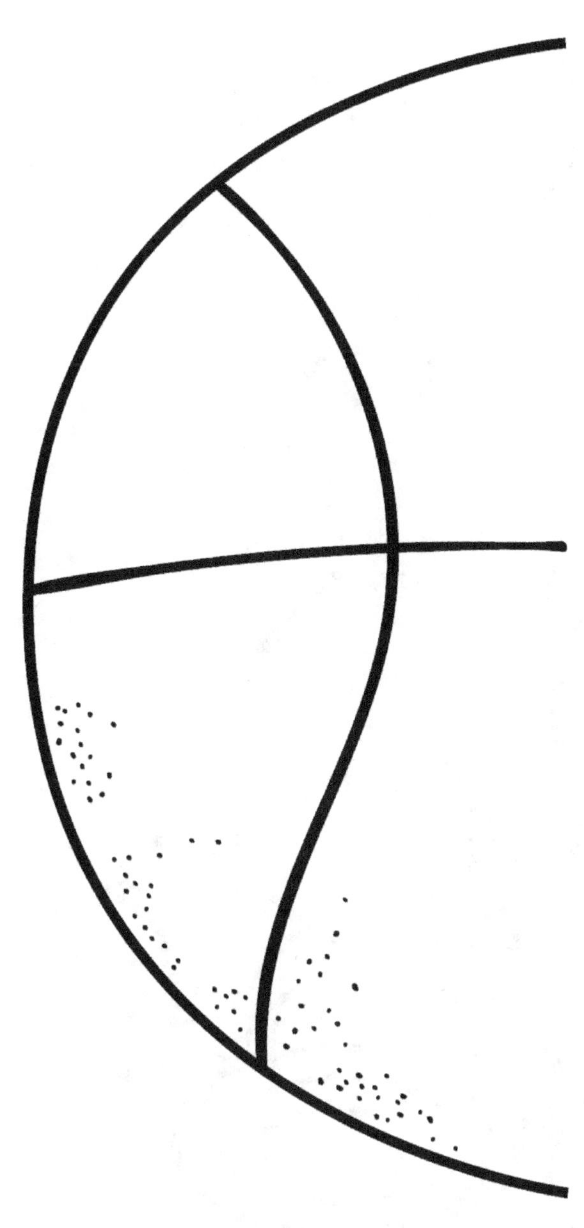

Shapes and Colors

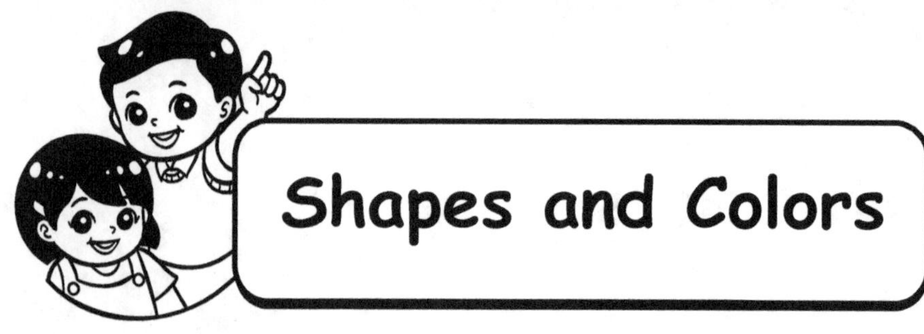

Orange

Crumple and tape orange Japanese paper to make fire.

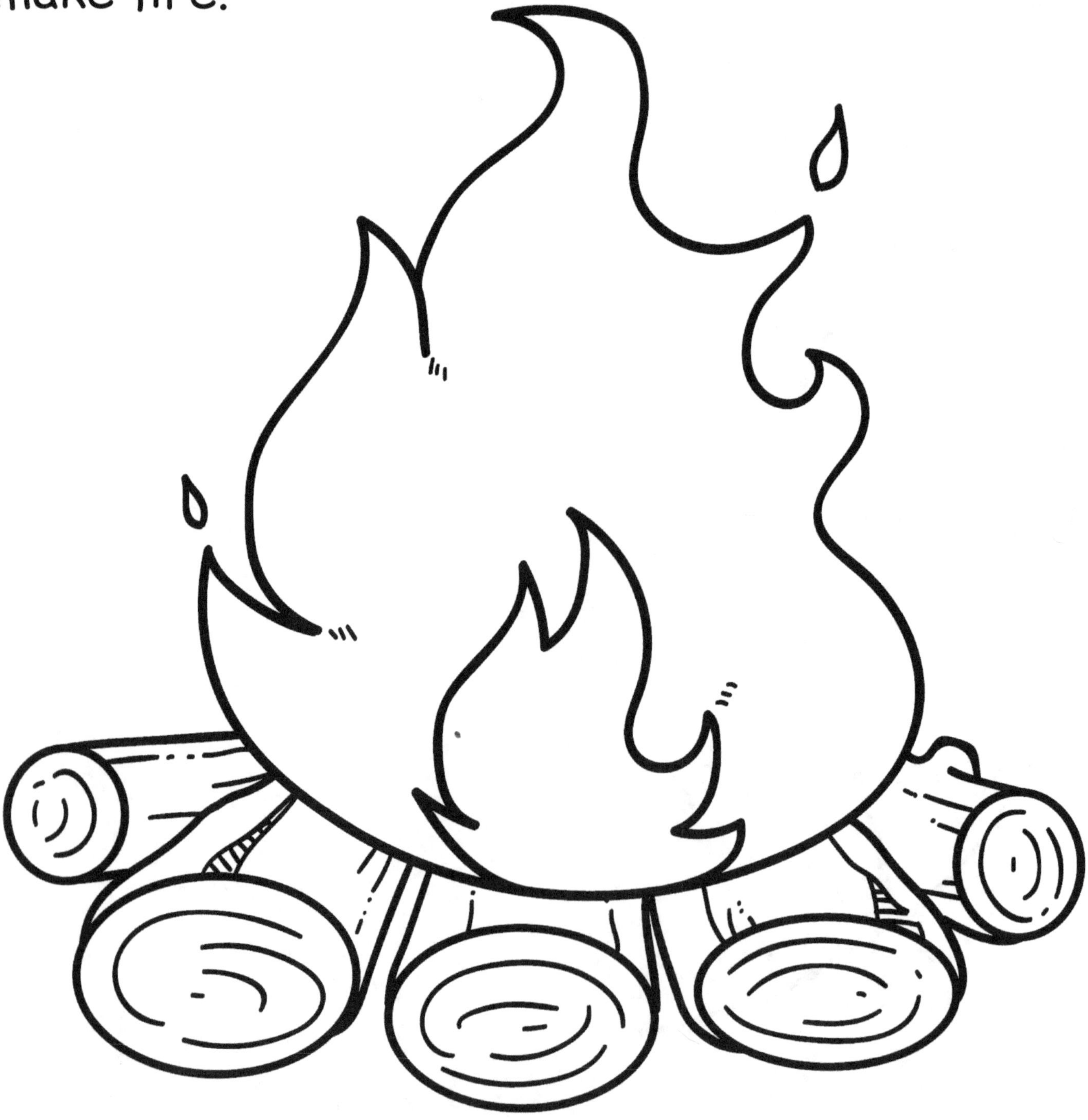

Skills: Crumpling; Pressing

Violet

Use violet paint to make an eggplant.

Shapes and Colors

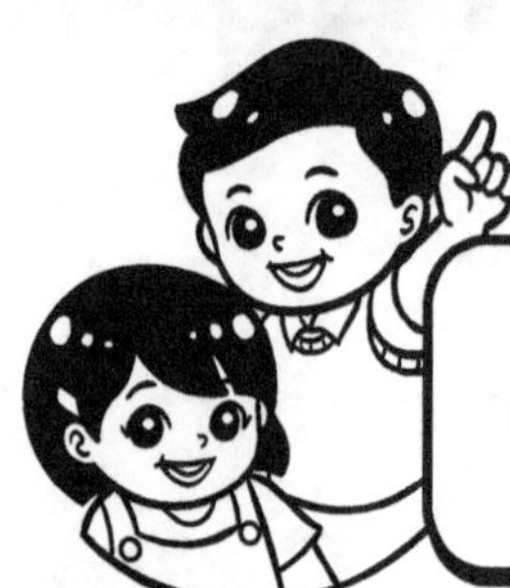

Violet

Drip violet paint on onion halves. Stamp them on the page.

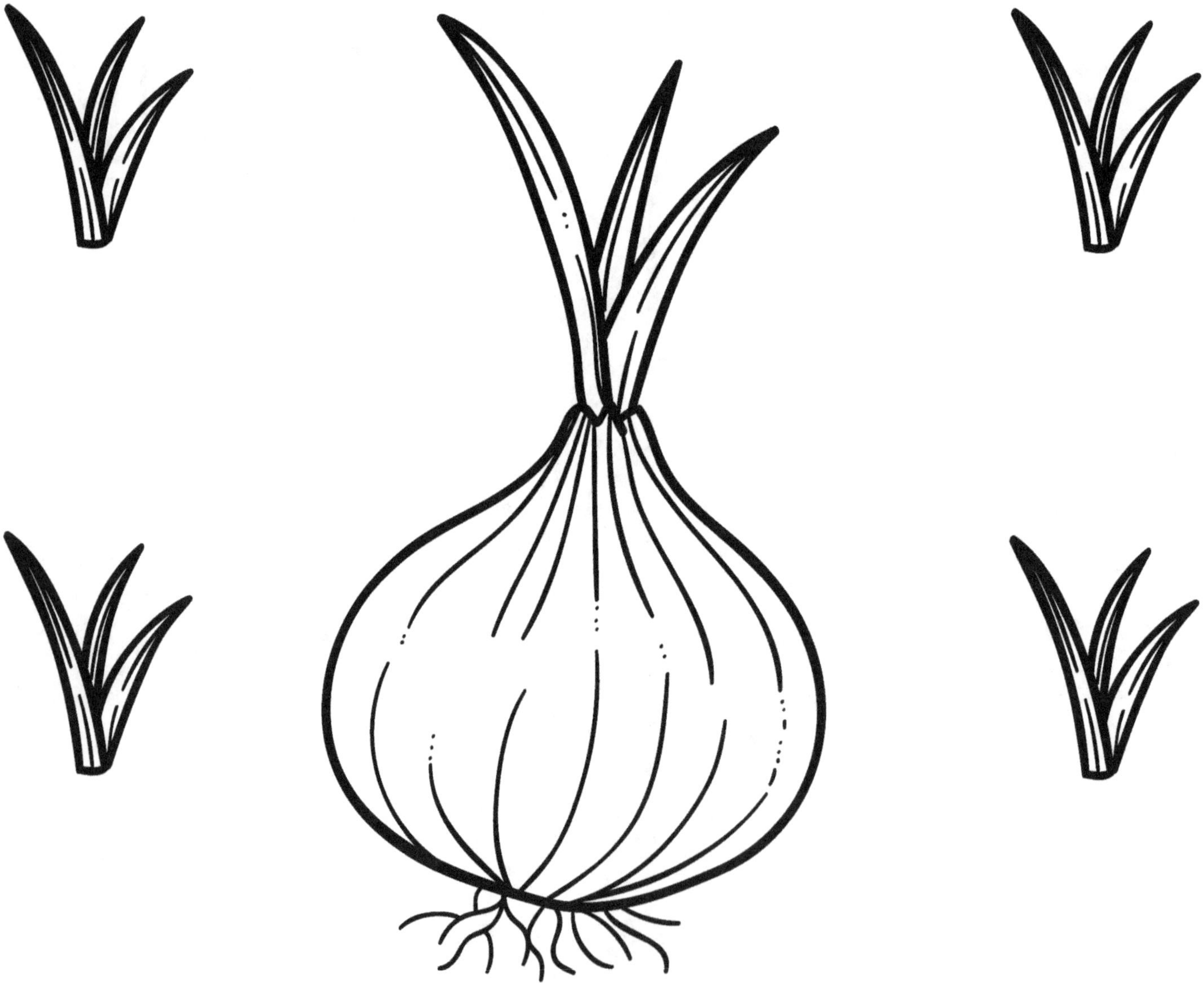

Skills: Stamping

Shapes and Colors

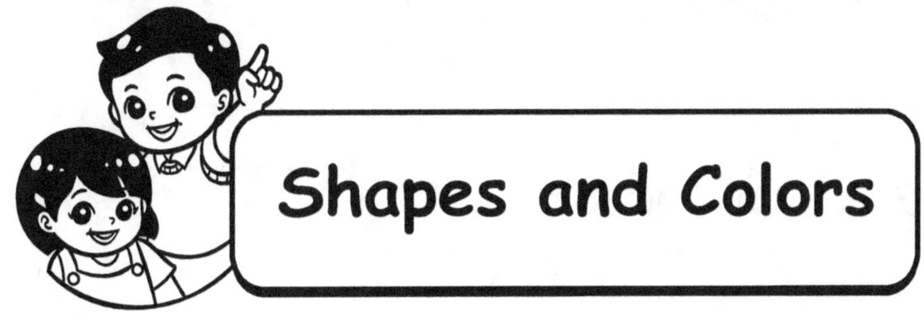

Brown

Glue brown yarn to make the horse's mane and tail. Color the picture after.

Skills: Pasting; Coloring

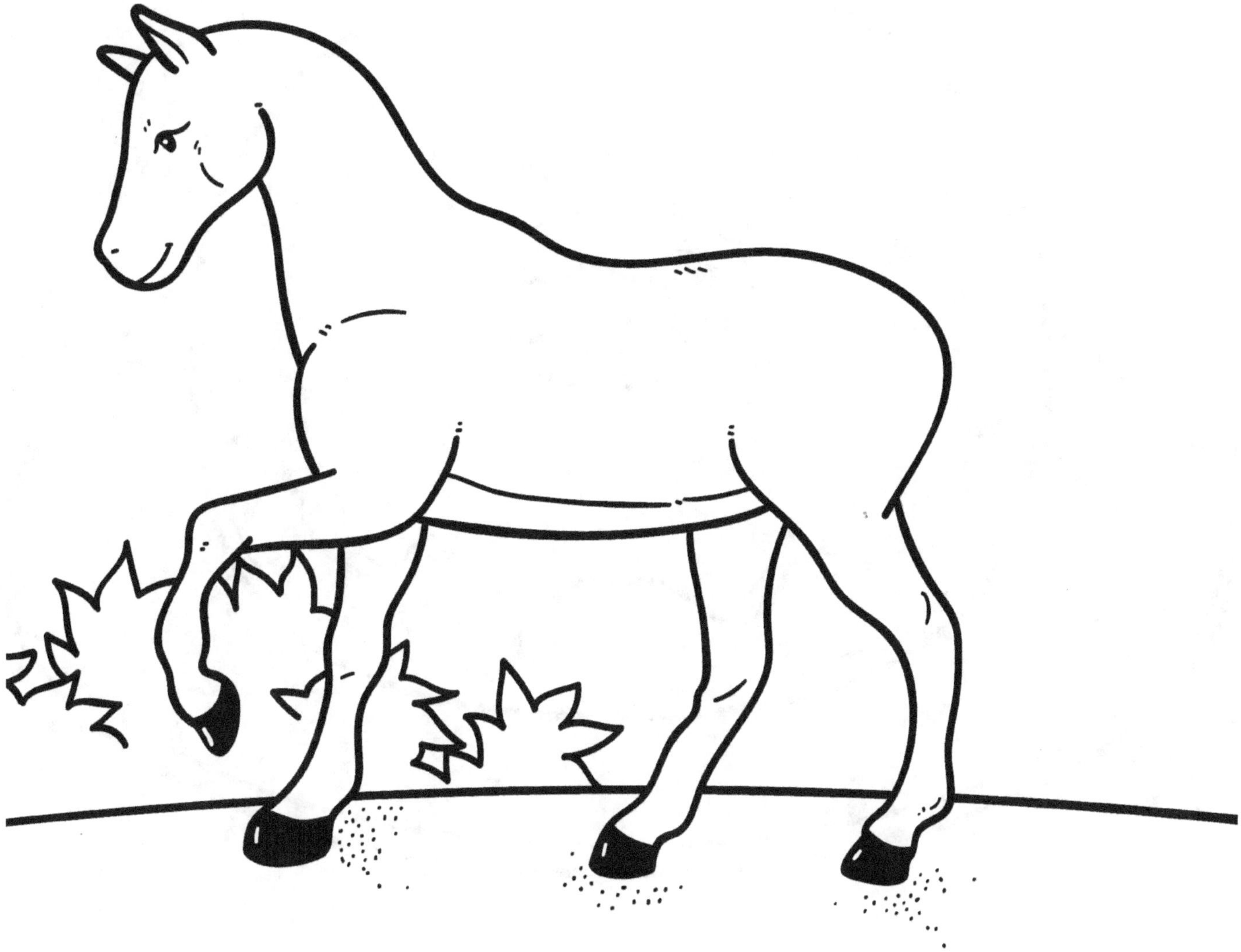

Shapes and Colors

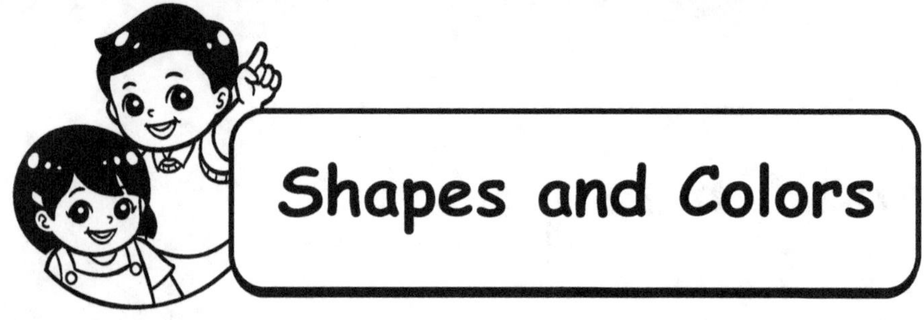

Brown

Spread glue on the donut. Sprinkle coffee powder after.

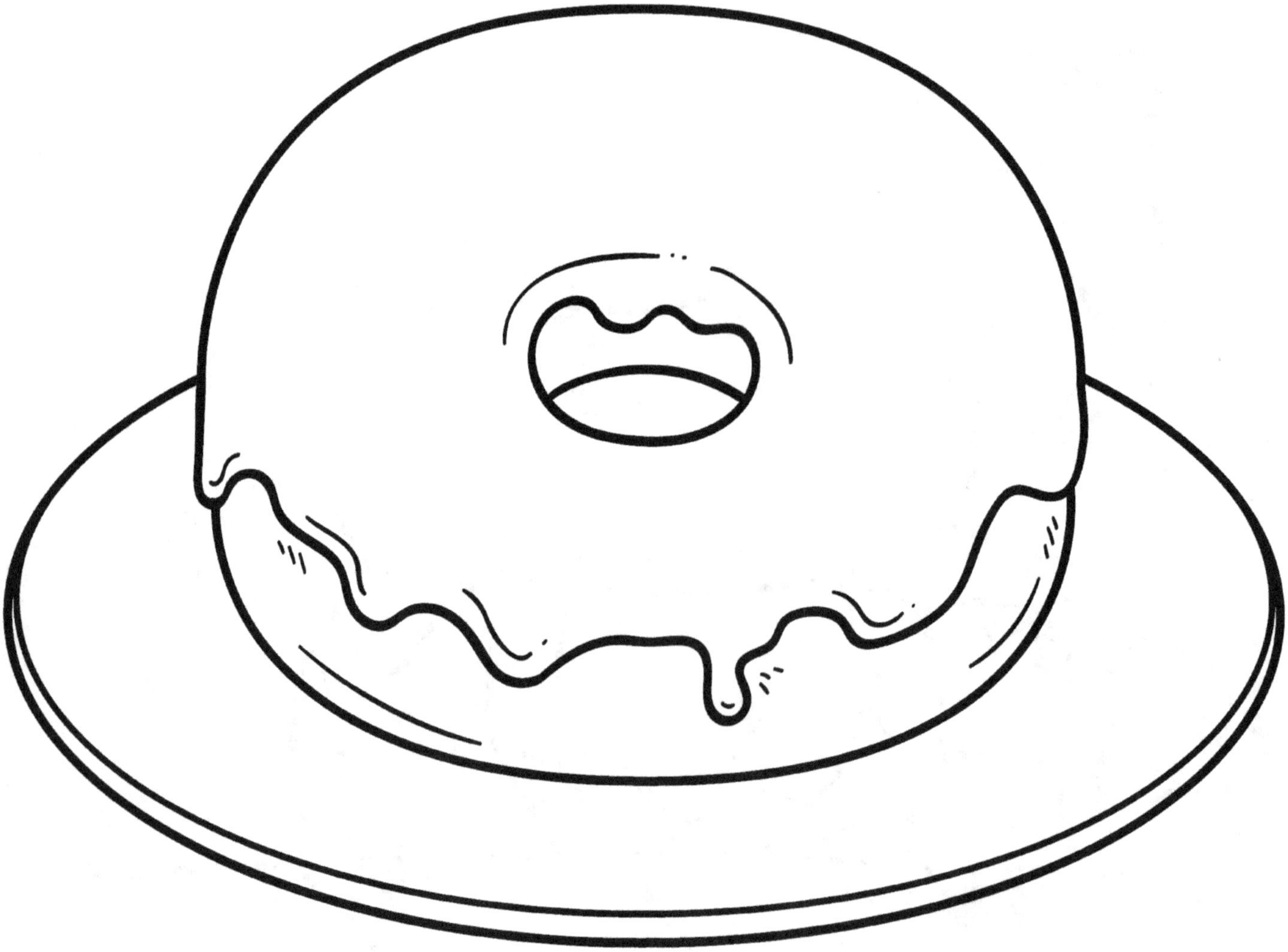

Skills: Brushing; Fine Motor

Black

Dip your thumb on black paint. Stamp it 4 times above each black circle to make paw prints.

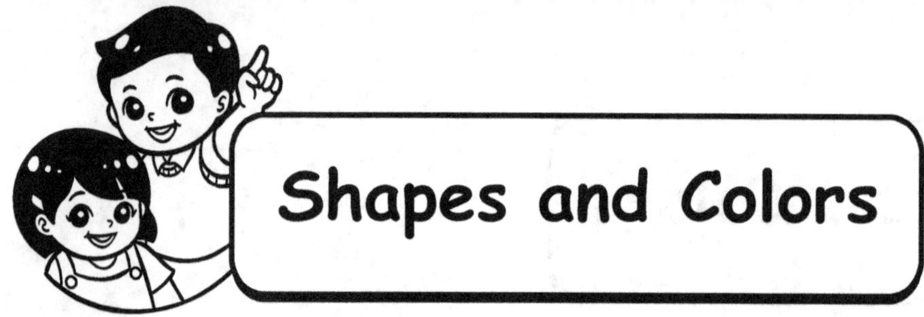

Black

Cut and paste black strips of paper on the picture to make a zebra.

Skills: Cutting; Pasting

Shapes and Colors

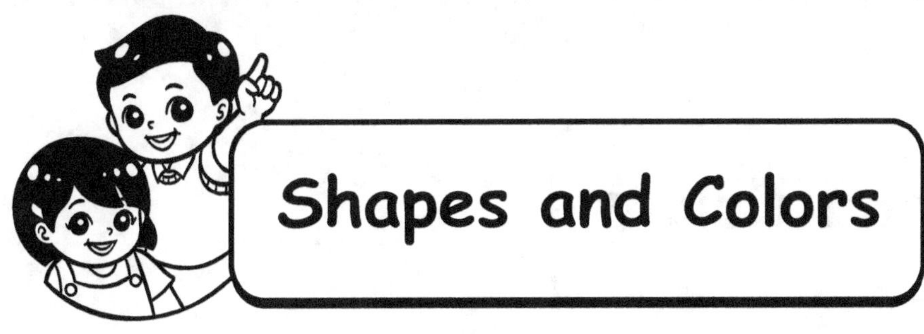

Pink

Put pink buttons on the pigs' faces. Use glue to attach the pink buttons.

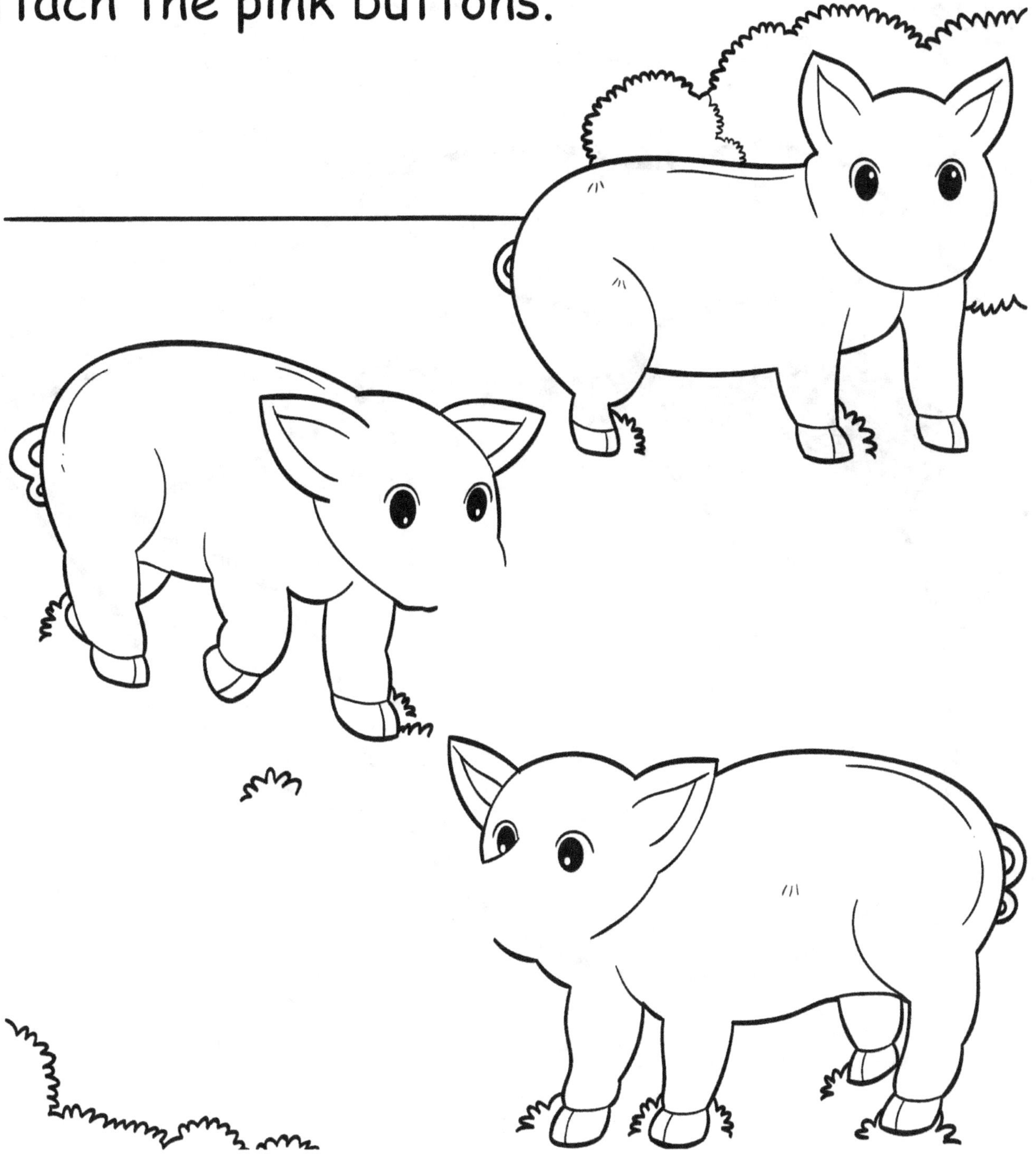

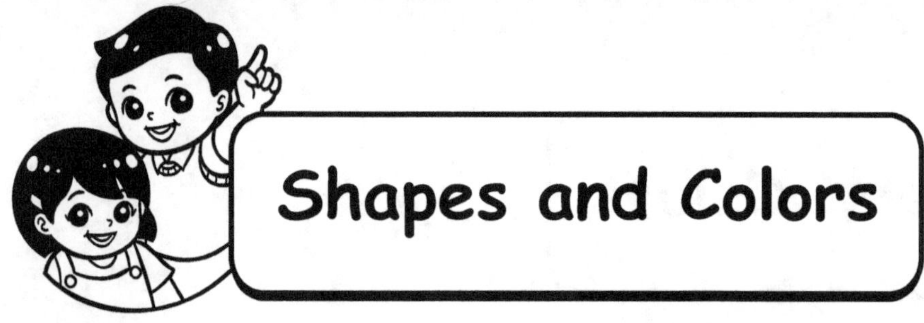

Pink

Dip the cotton bud on pink paint. Dab and fill the tongue.

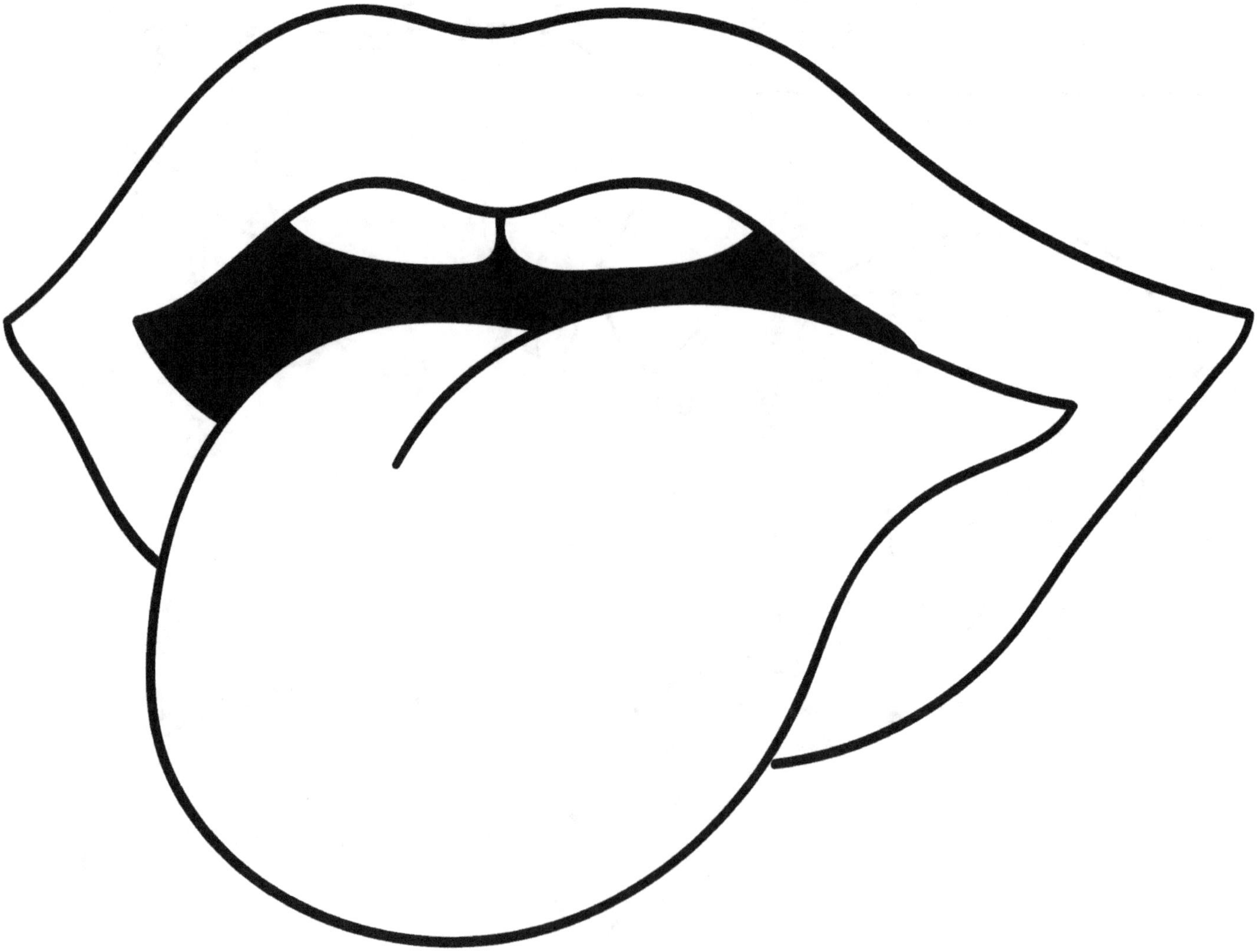

Skills: Dabbing

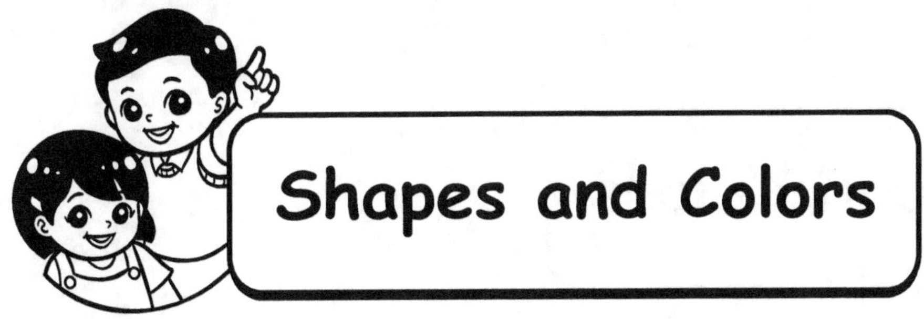

White

Paste pieces of white crumpled paper to make popcorn.

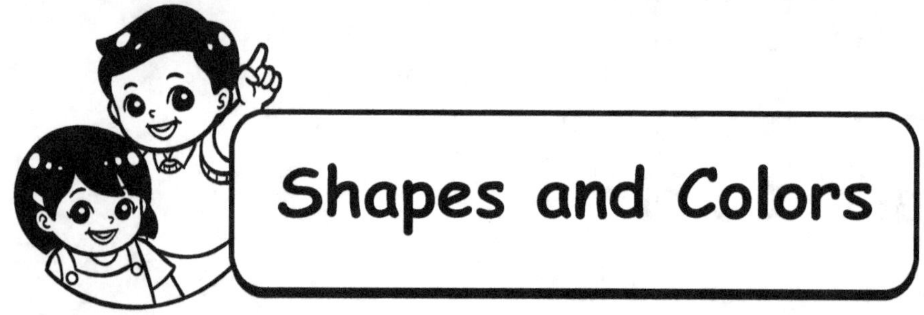

White

Drip white paint and sprinkle salt after to make soap suds.

Skills: Fine Motor

Textures and Surfaces

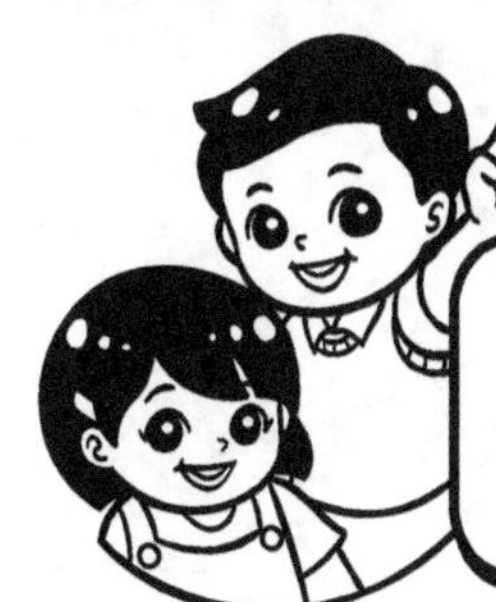

Soft

Paste cotton on the rabbit.

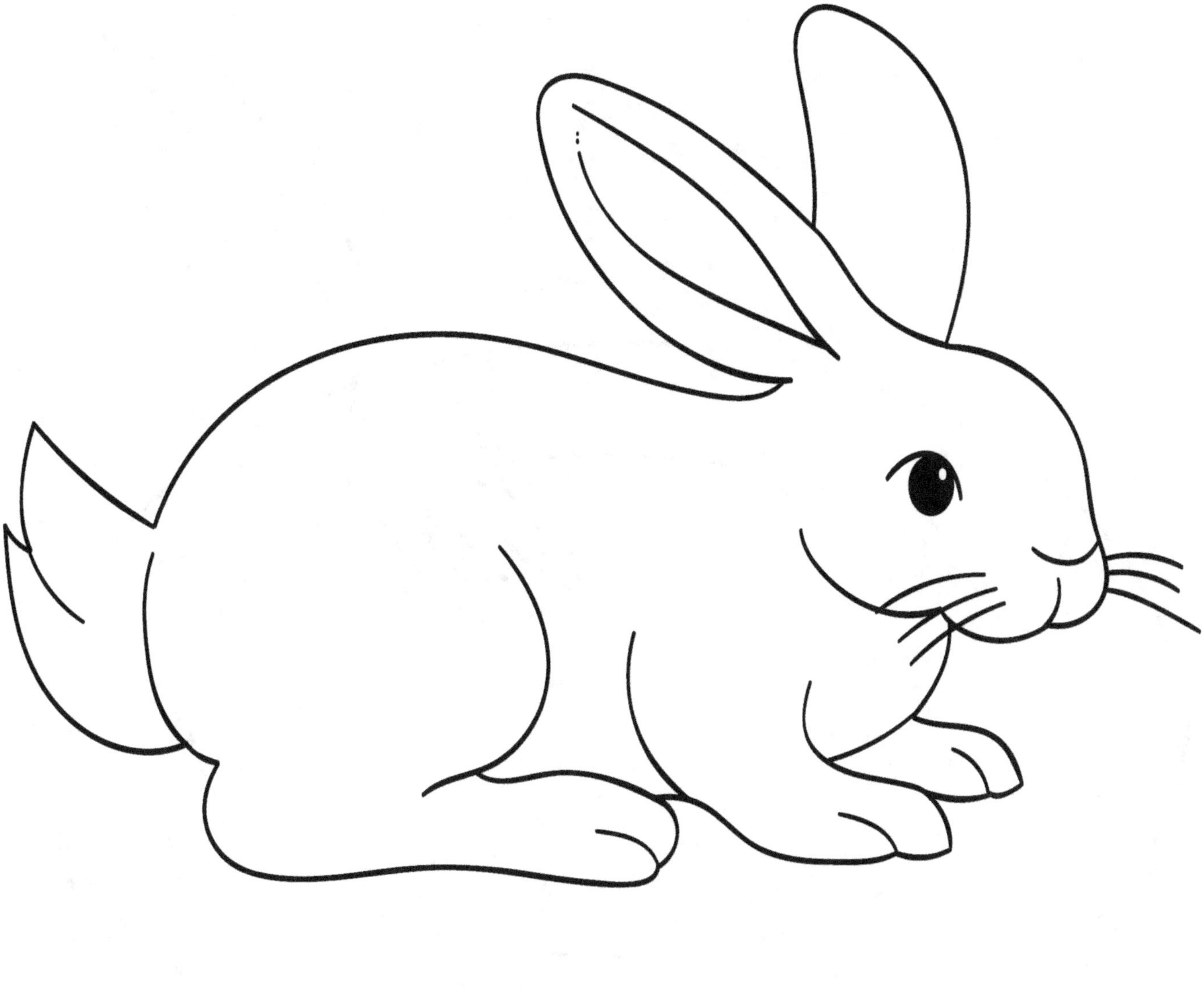

Textures and Surfaces

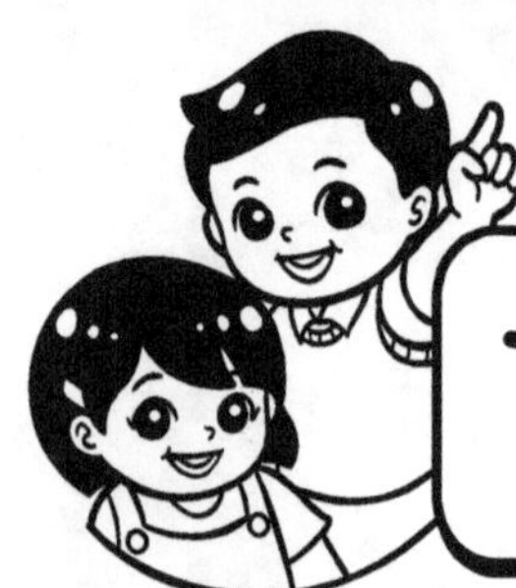

Soft

Paste red and orange yarn on the plate to make pasta.

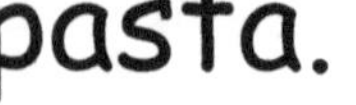

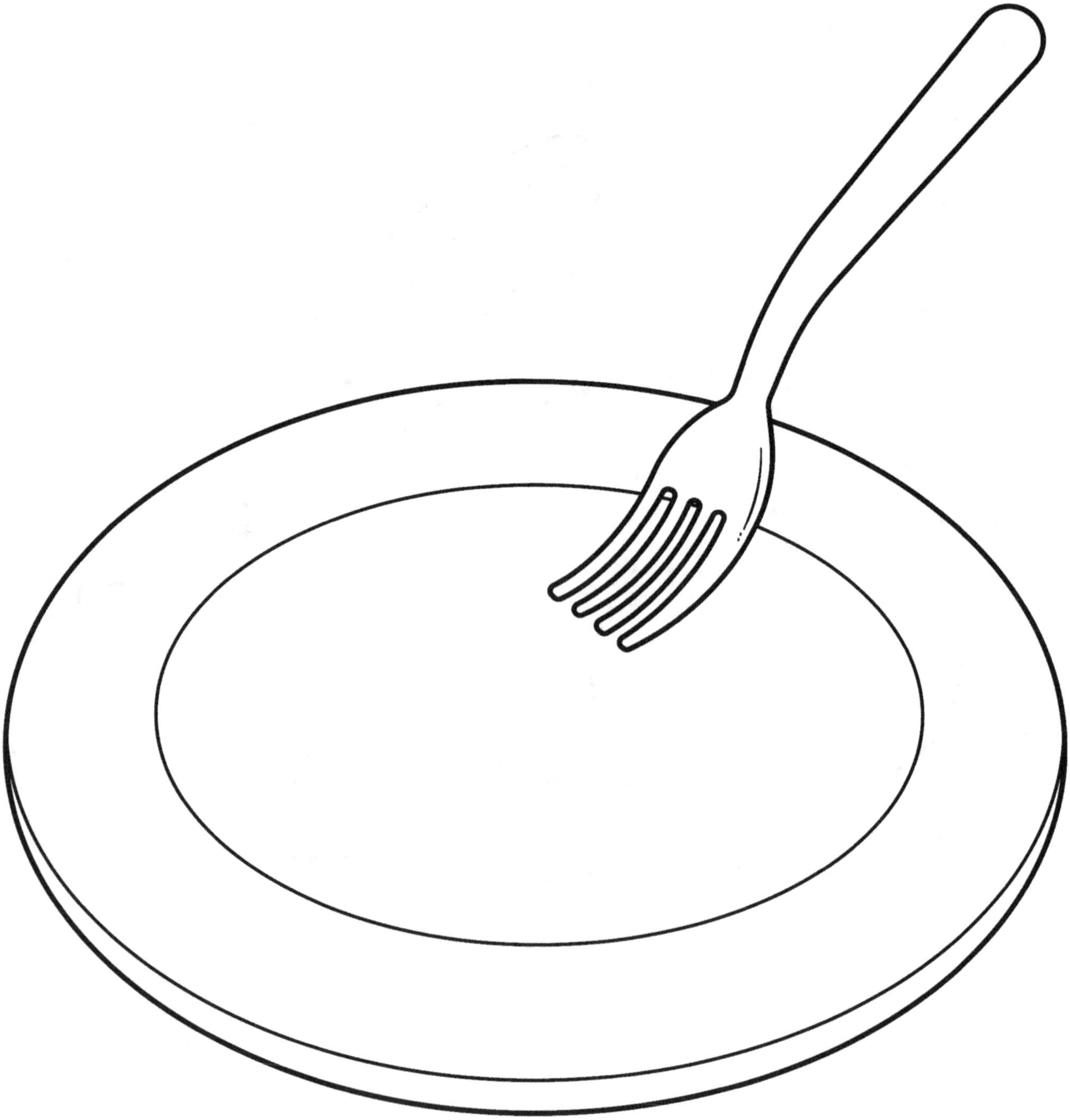

Skills: Pasting; Cutting

Soft

Paste different colored yarns to make a shaved ice dessert.

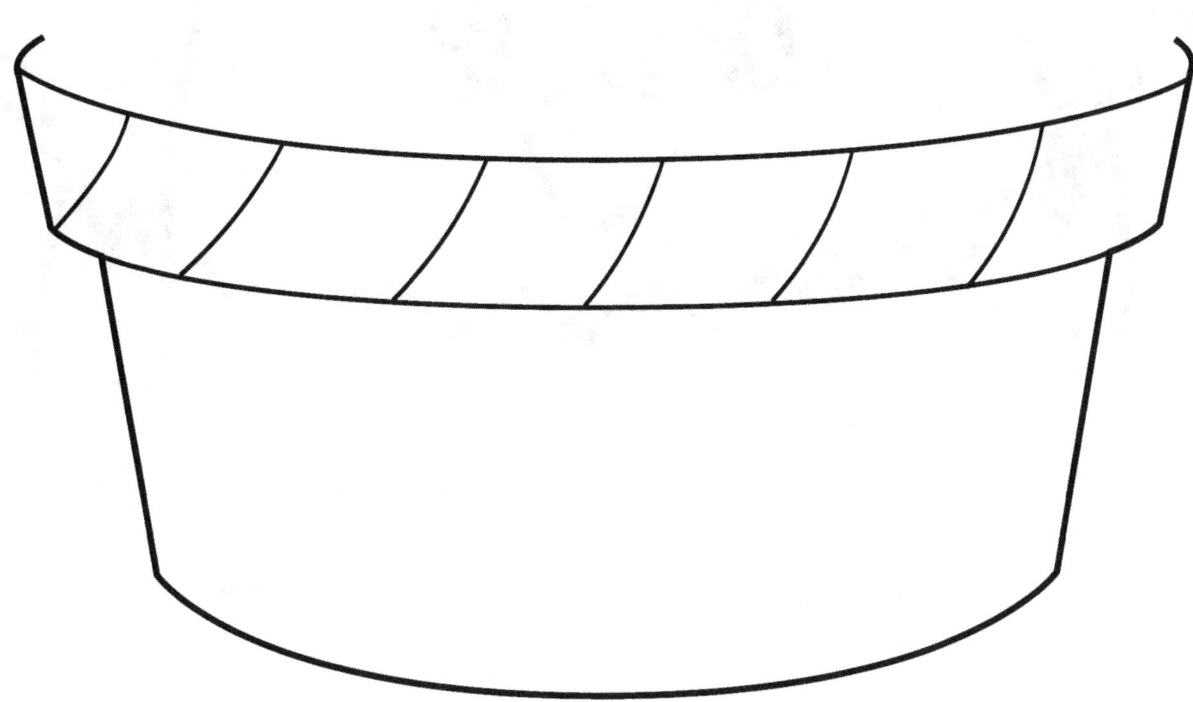

Rough

Paste crushed eggshells to complete the picture.

Skills: Fine Motor; Pasting

Rough

Paste a strip of sandpaper to make a bookmark.

Put the sandpaper here.

Textures and Surfaces

Hard

Glue popsicle sticks to make the bodies.

Skills: Pressing

Textures and Surfaces

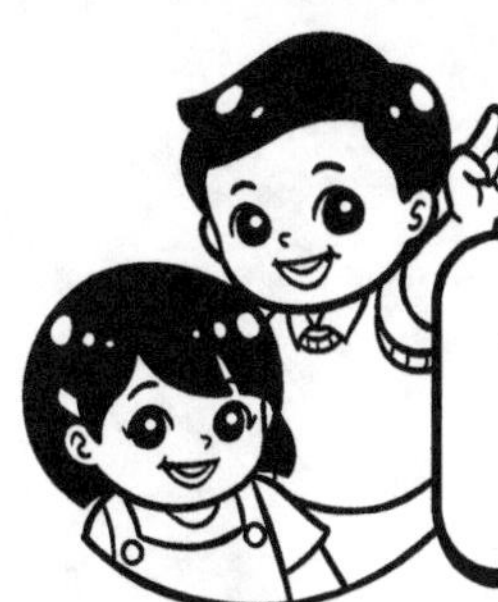

Hard

Paste different buttons to decorate the shell.

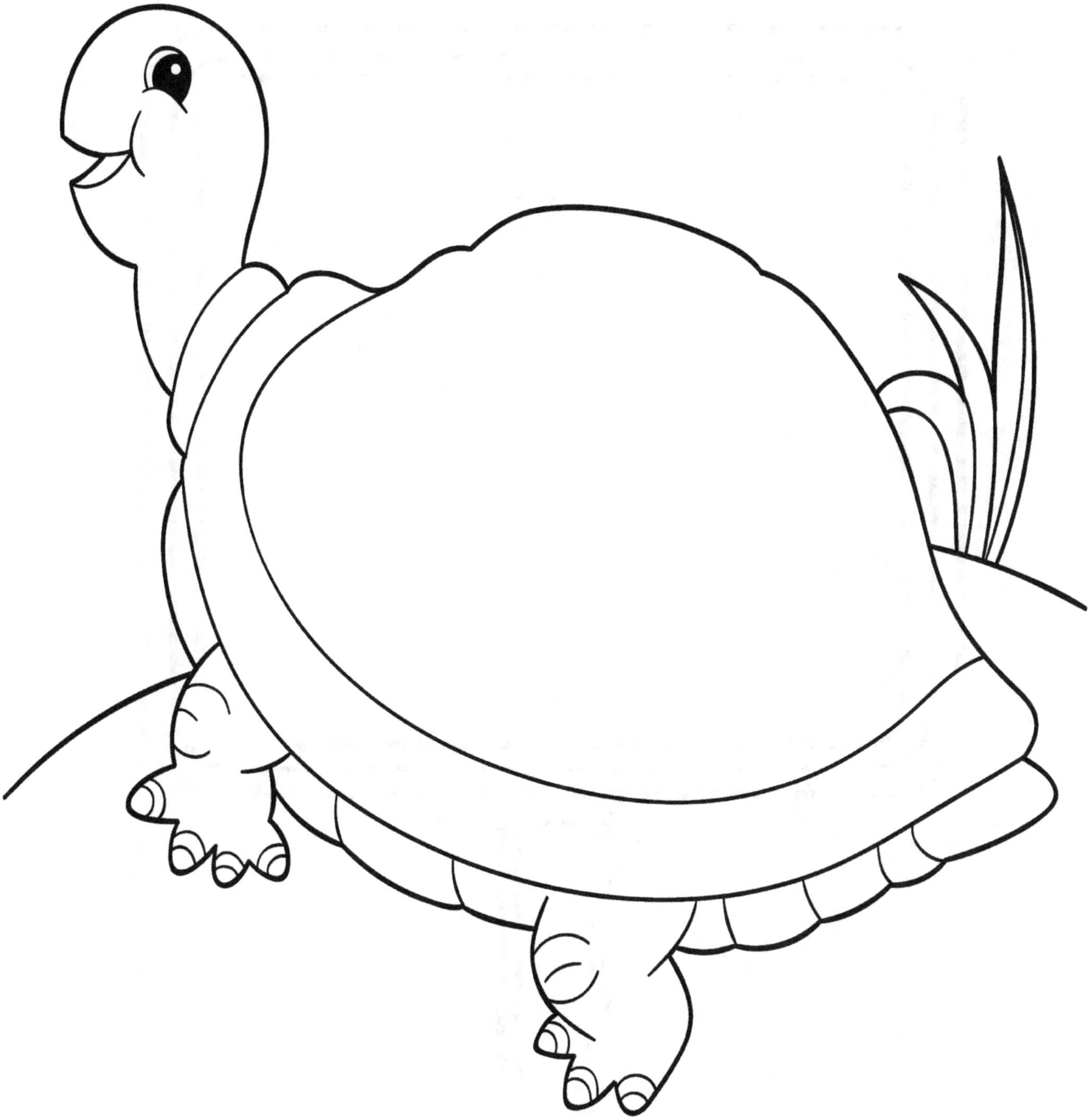

Textures and Surfaces

Smooth

Tape any transparent recycled plastic cover on the mirror frame.

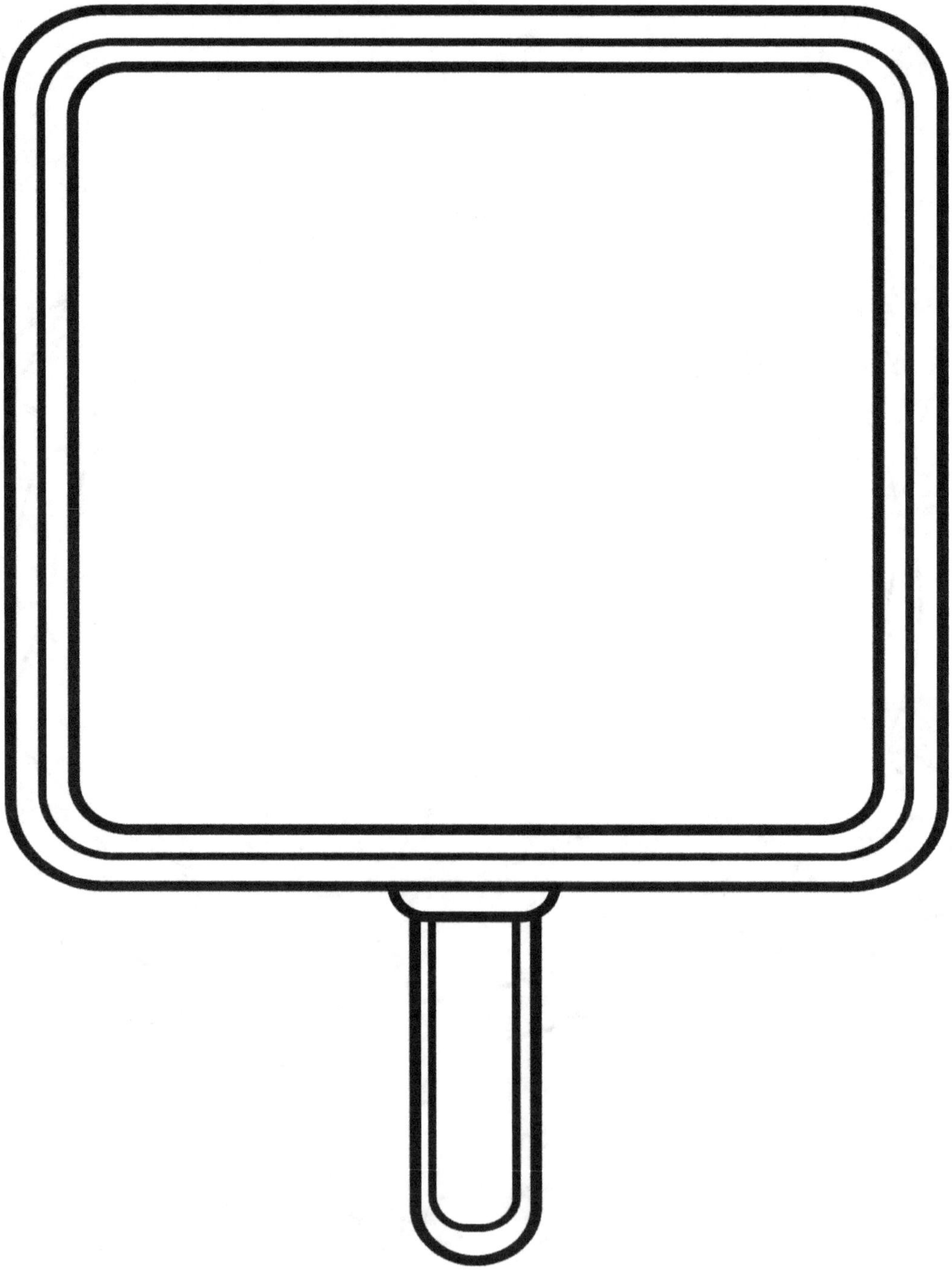

Skills: Pasting; Recycling

Textures and Surfaces

Smooth

Squeeze glue on the pearls. Let it dry.

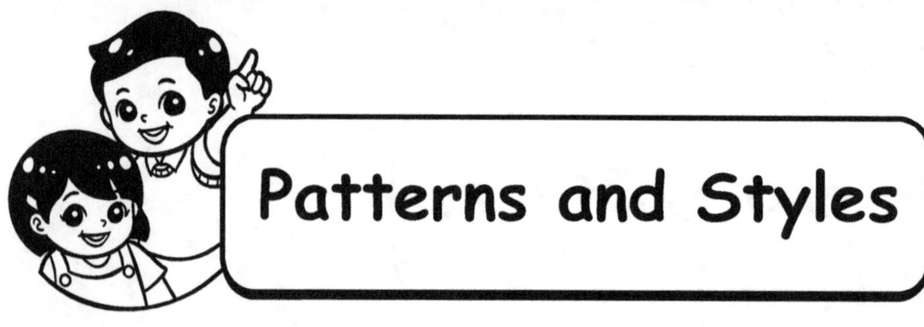

Line pattern
Complete the line patterns.

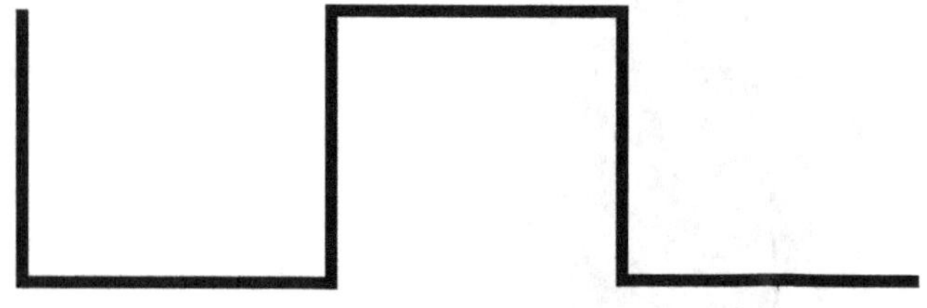

Skills: Writing; Cognition

Patterns and Styles

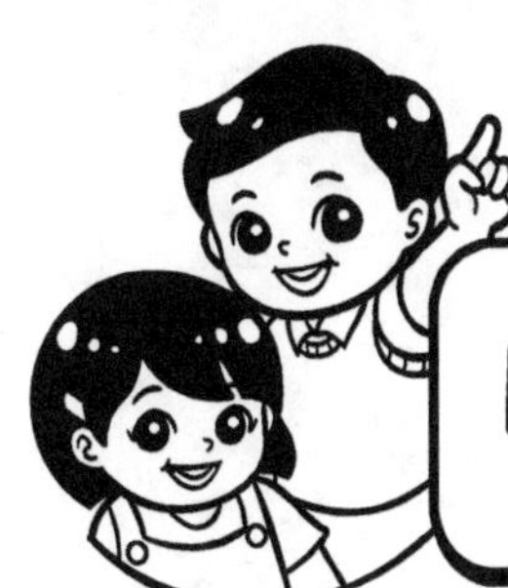

Line pattern

Draw line patterns to complete the picture.

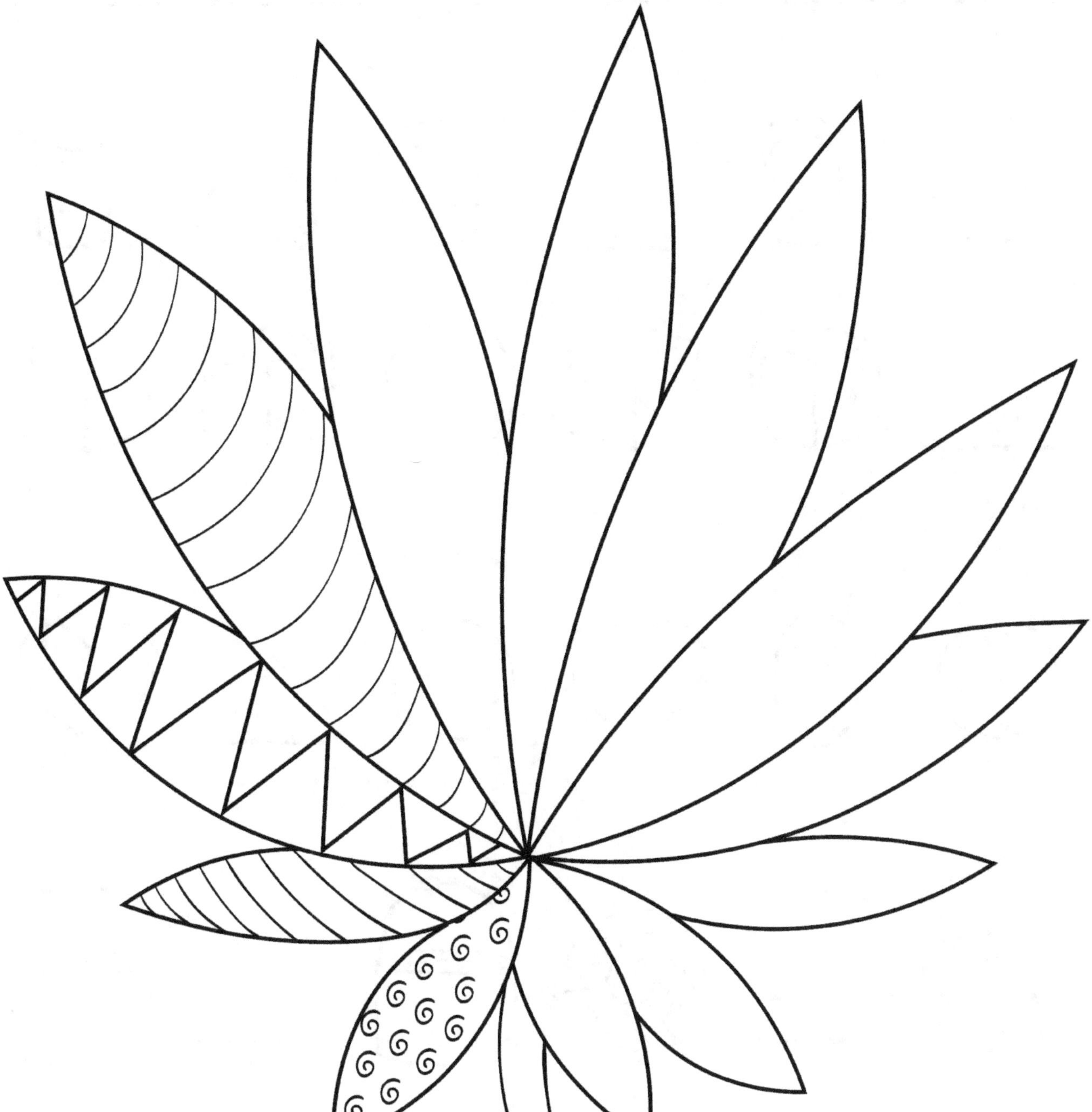

Skills: Drawing; Cognition

Patterns and Styles

Shape pattern
Draw the missing shape/s of each pattern.

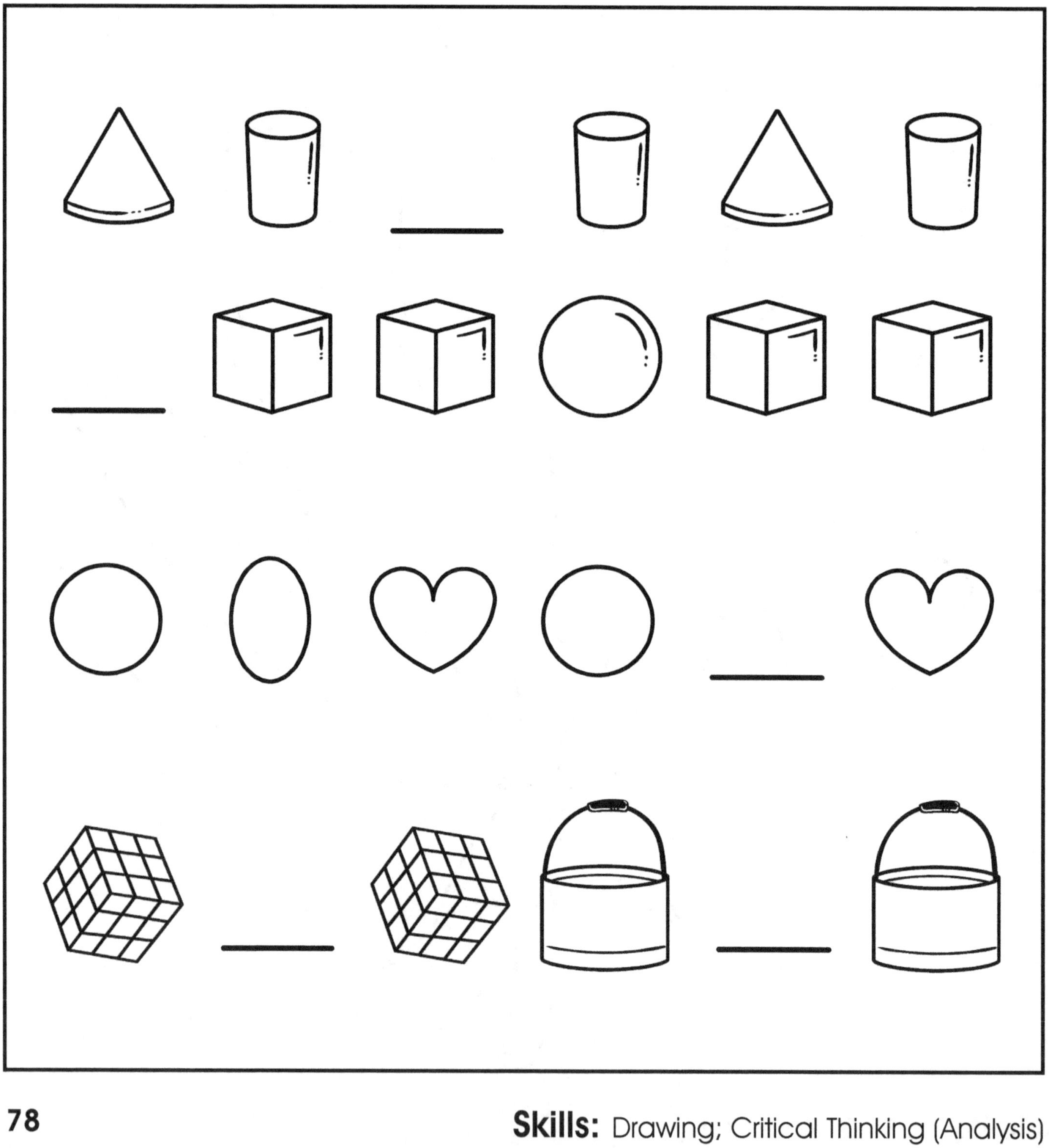

Skills: Drawing; Critical Thinking (Analysis)

Patterns and Styles

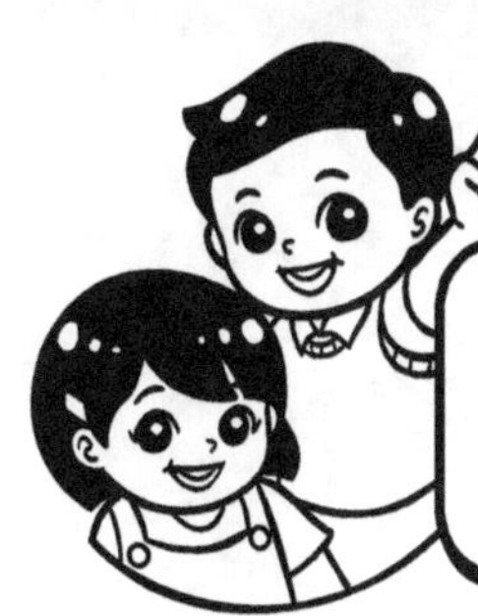

Shape pattern

Draw shapes to make a pattern.

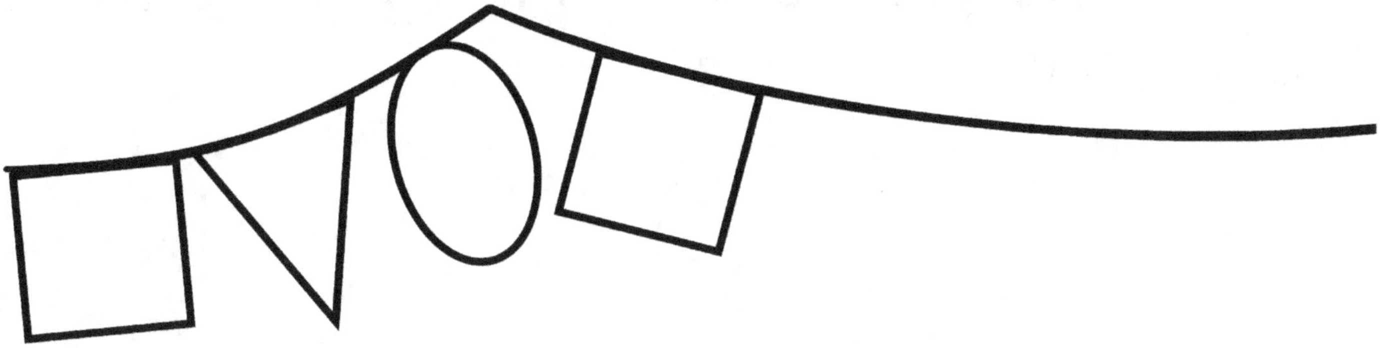

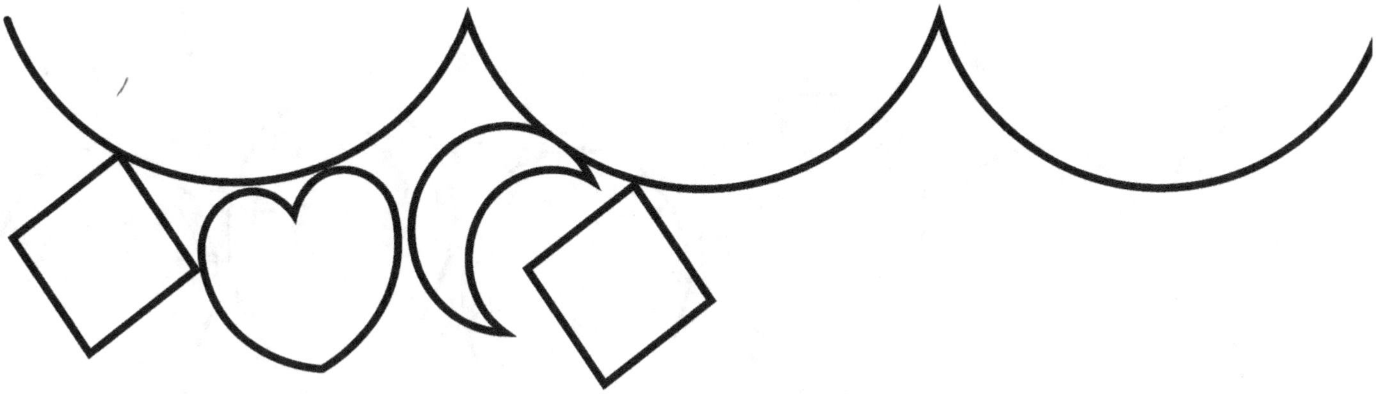

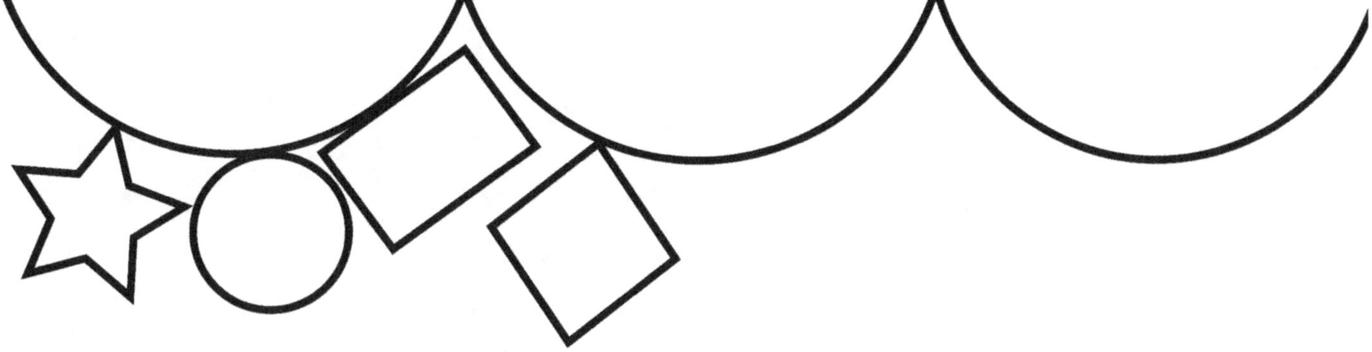

Patterns and Styles

Color pattern

What is the color of the mangoes when it is ripe and unripe? Color the mangoes to make that pattern.

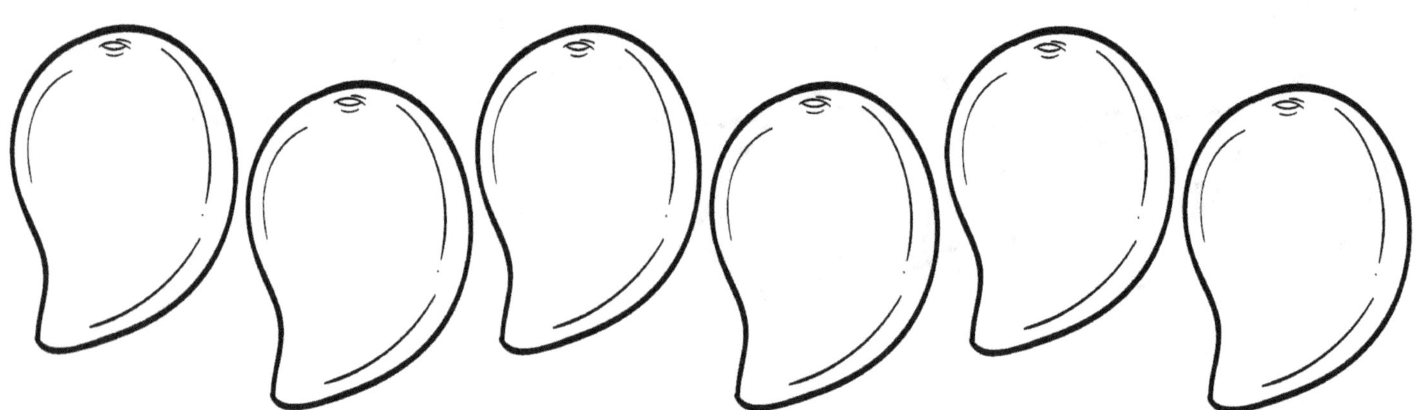

Skills: Coloring; Critical Thinking (Application)

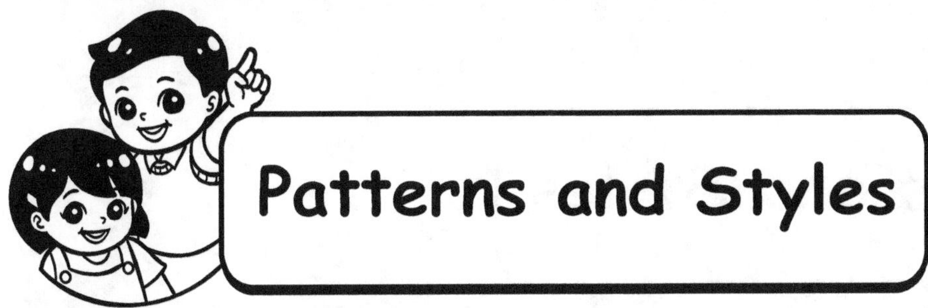

Shape pattern

Draw shapes to make a pattern.

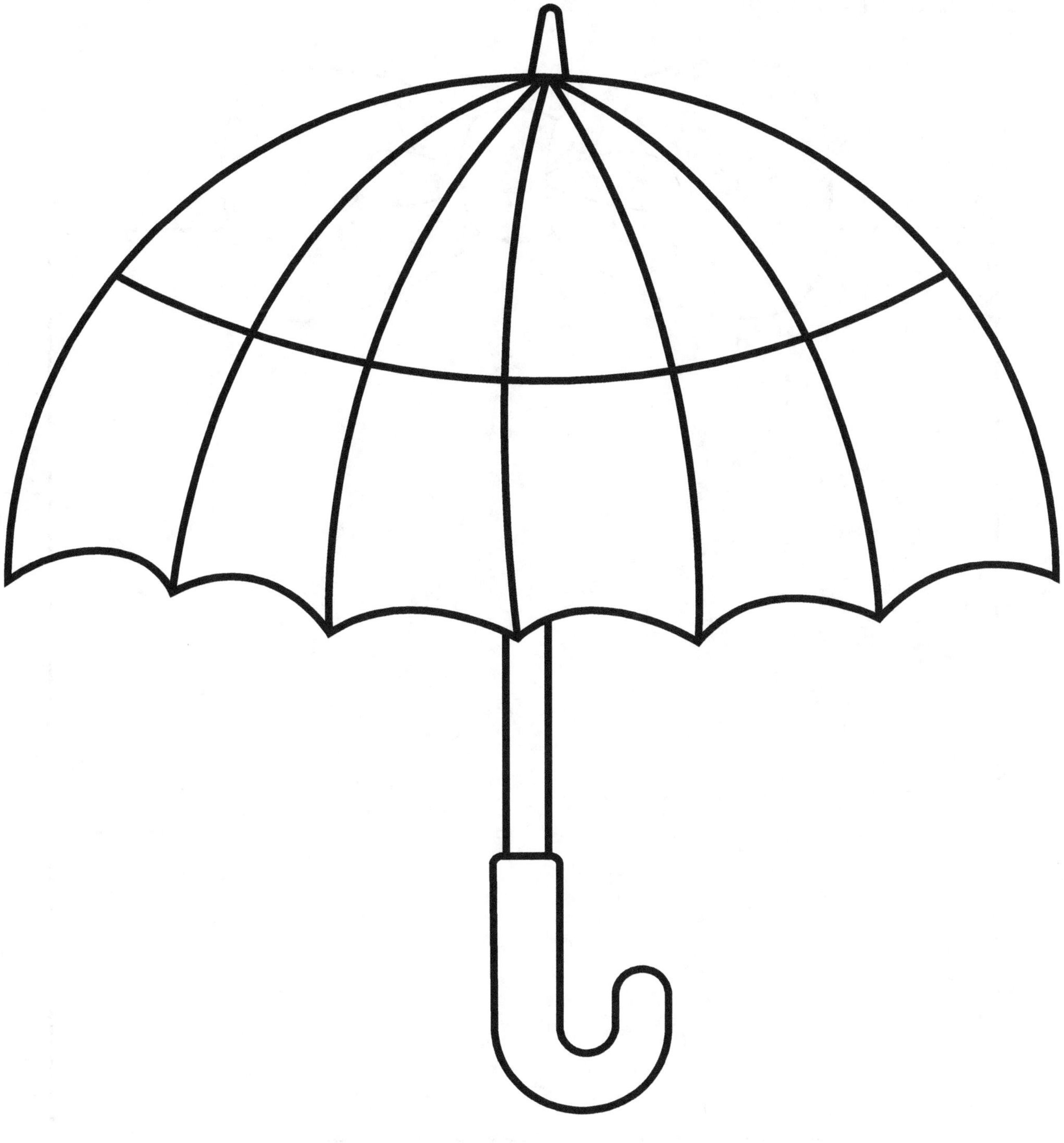

Patterns and Styles

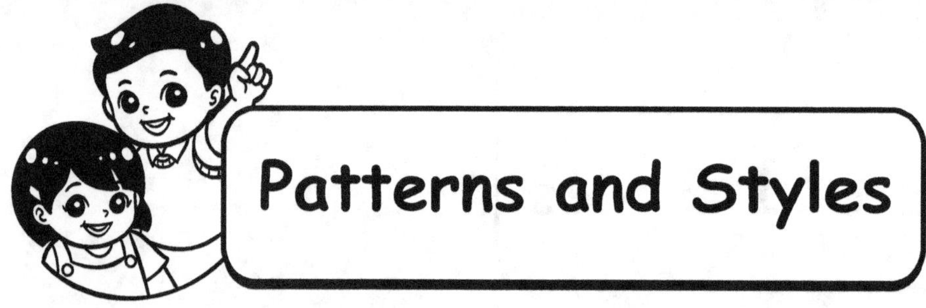

Line and color patterns

Design the gift by making your own line and color patterns.

Skills: Drawing; Coloring; Critical Thinking (Synthesis)

Mother's day

Color and cut the paper to make bracelets for mother.

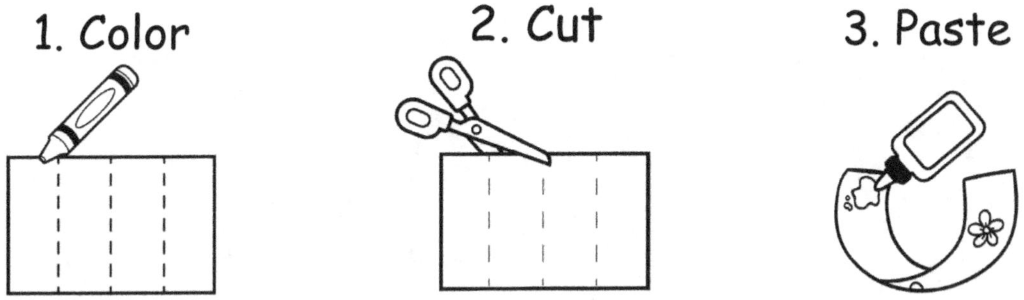

1. Color   **2. Cut**   **3. Paste**

Special Occasions

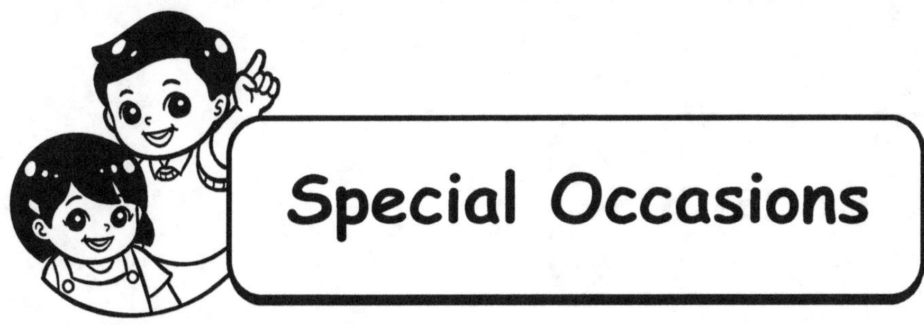

Father's day

Trace the heart and draw patterns on the tie.

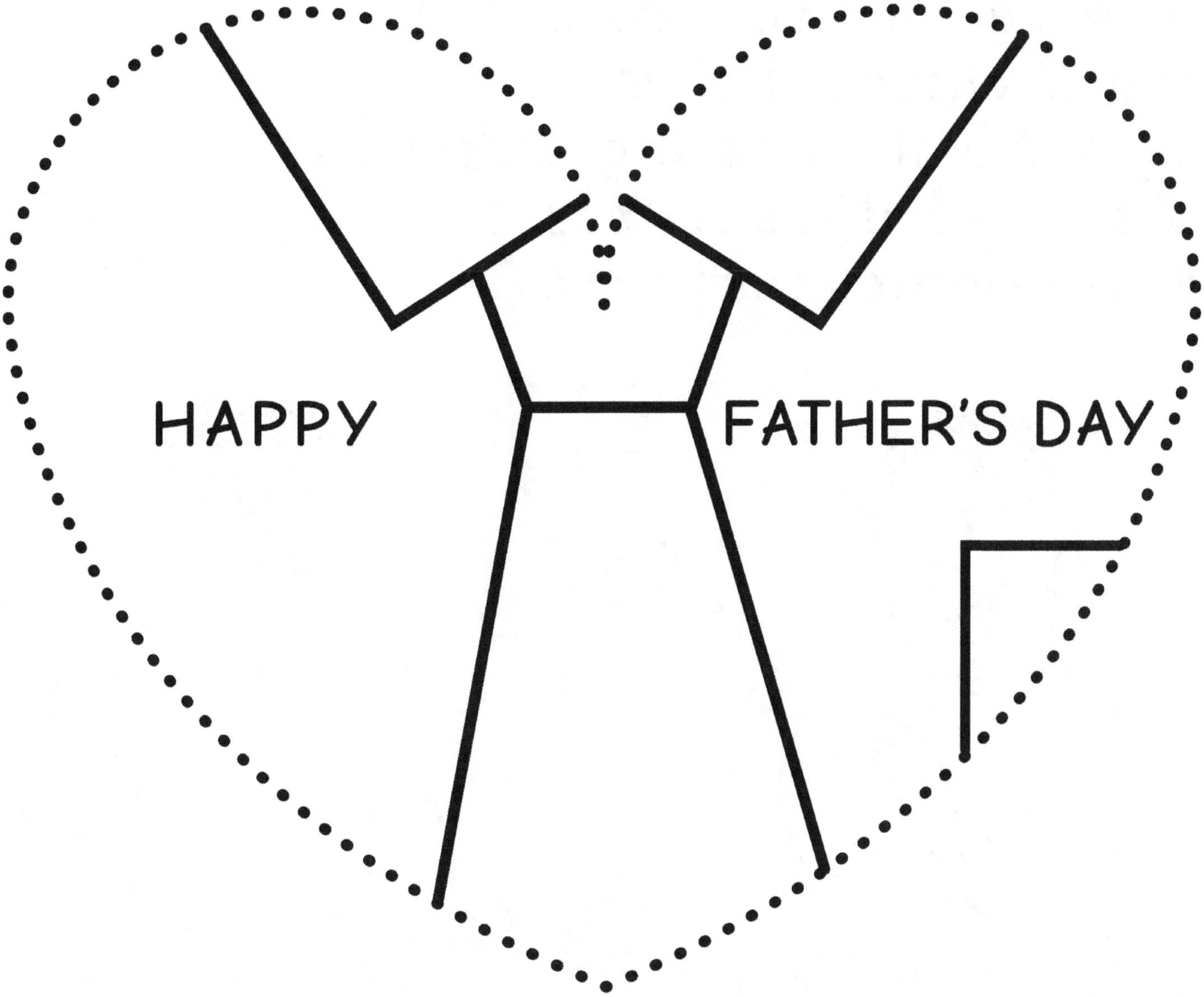

Special Occasions

Grandparents' Day

Color the grandparents using the color code below.

Gray: hair and moustache

Red: Grandpa's clothes

Light Brown: faces of grandparents

Green: Grandma's clothes

Your favorite color: words

Skills: Coloring; Critical Thinking (Application)

Earth Day

Mold green, brown and blue clay to make a model of the Earth.

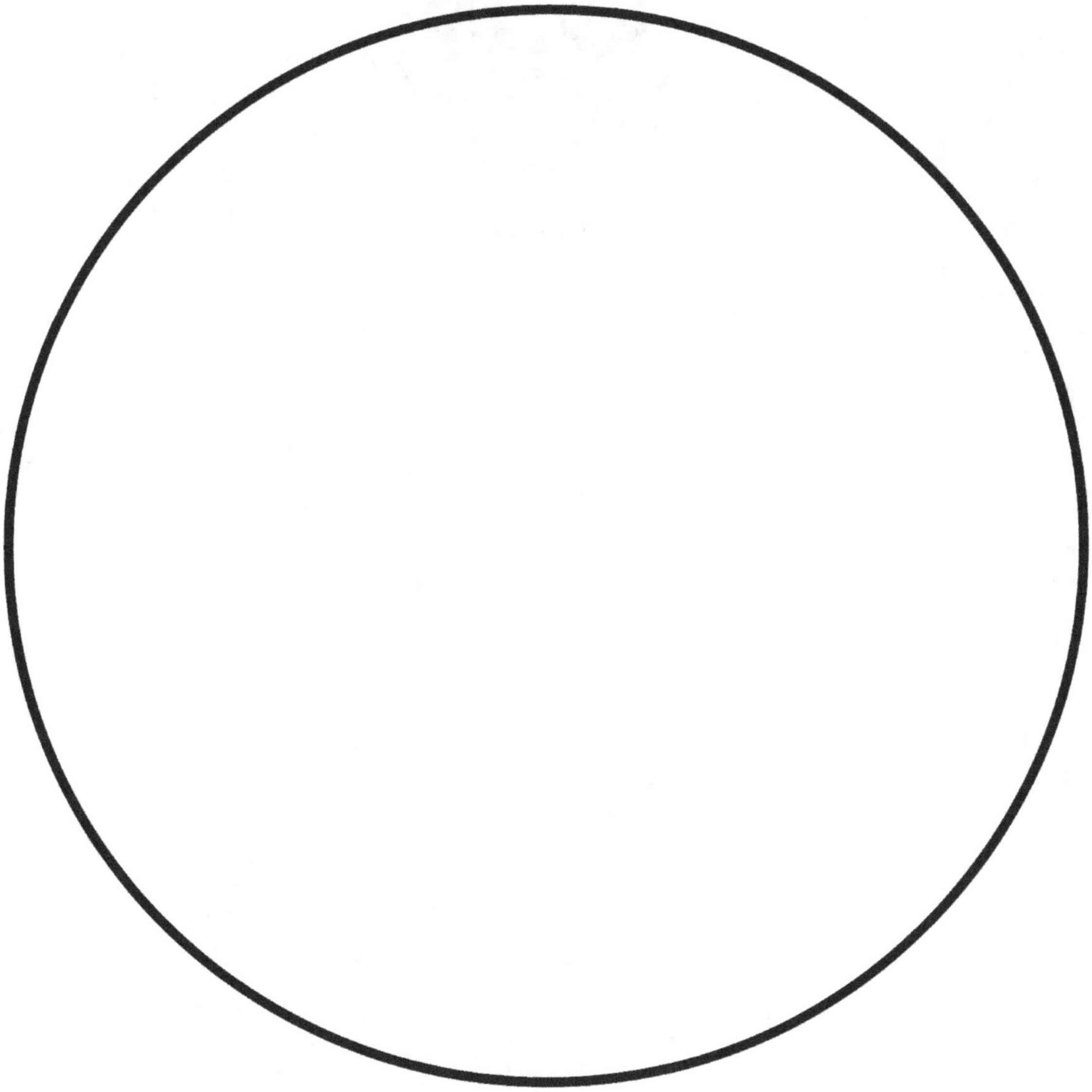

Halloween

Glue match sticks together to make a skeleton.

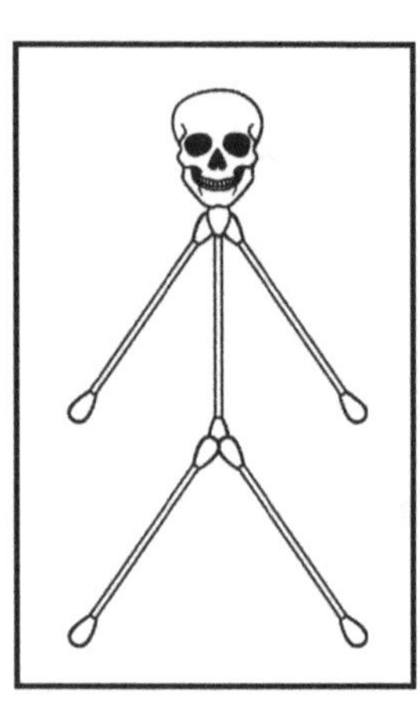

Skills: Pressing; Critical Thinking (Application)

Special Occasions

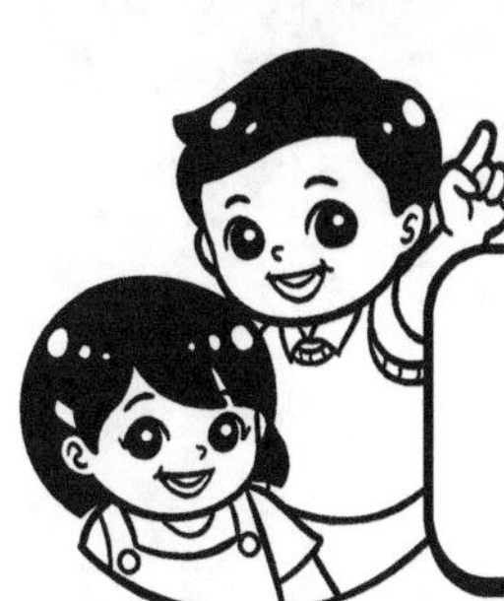

Christmas Day

Paste green and yellow crumpled crepe paper on the Christmas sock.

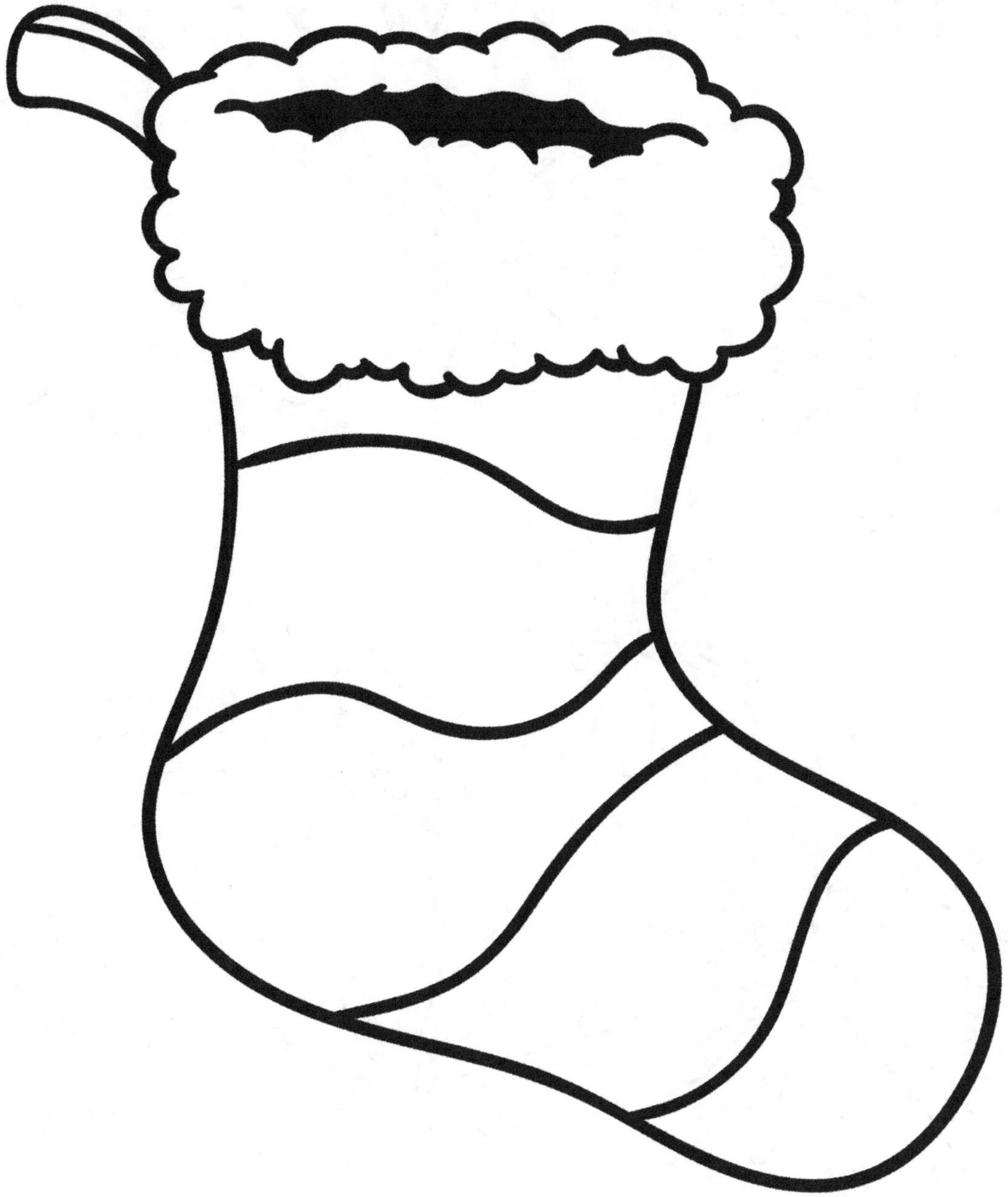

Special Occasions

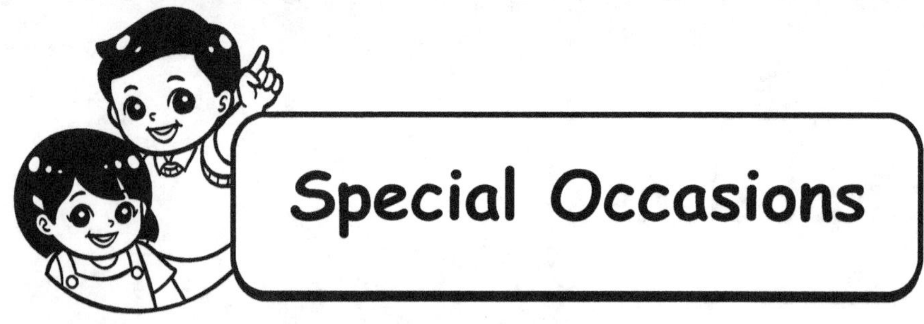

New Year's Day

Color the picture using different crayons. Brush black paint on the whole picture after.

HAPPY NEW YEAR!

Skills: Coloring; Painting

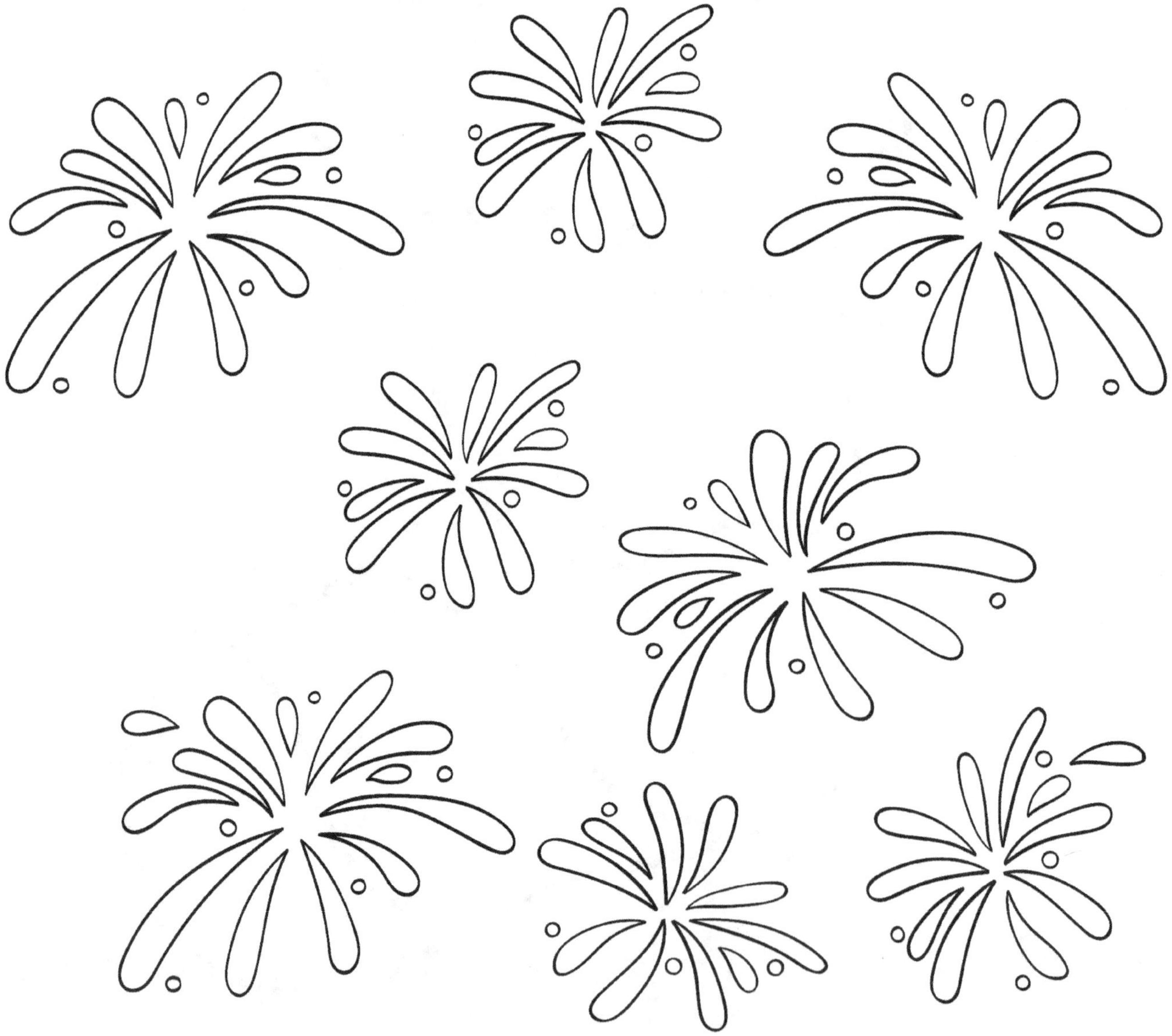

Special Occasions

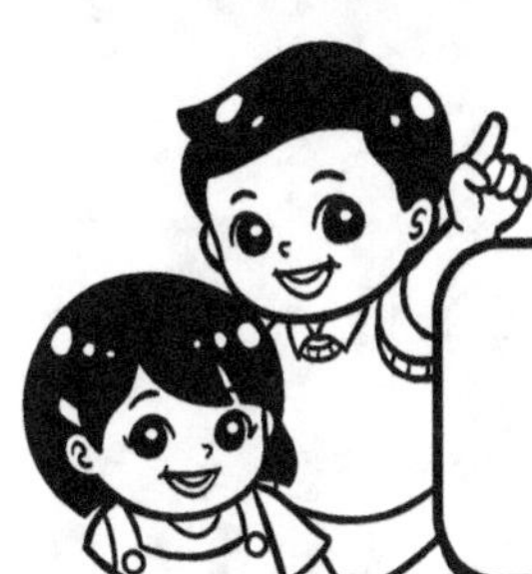

Valentine's Day

Cut pictures of flowers from old magazines. Paste the cutouts on the spaces below. Cut along the dotted lines to make a greeting card.

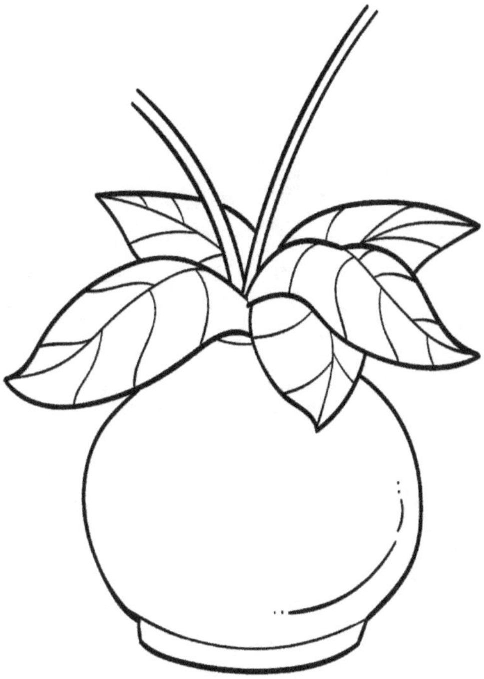

Skills: Cutting; Pasting

Copy and draw.

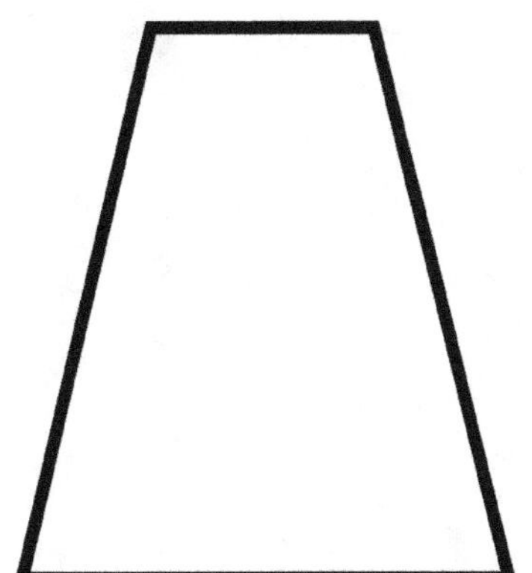

Art Application

Copy and draw.

Skills: Drawing; Critical Thinking (Application)

Copy and draw.

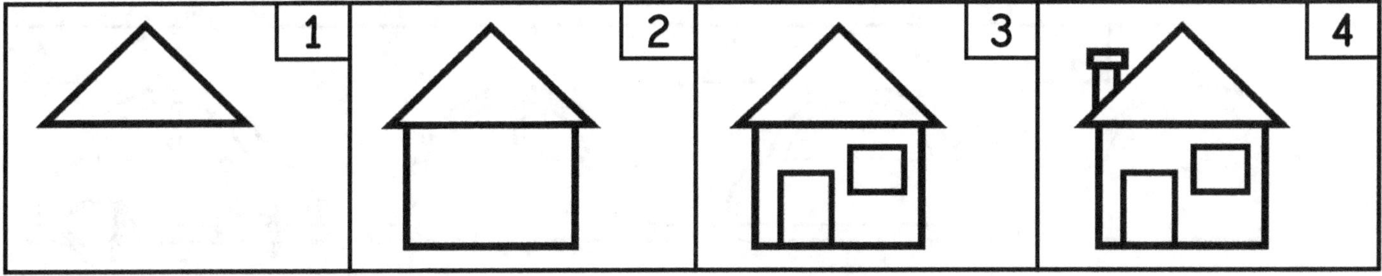

Skills: Drawing; Critical Thinking (Application)

Copy and draw.

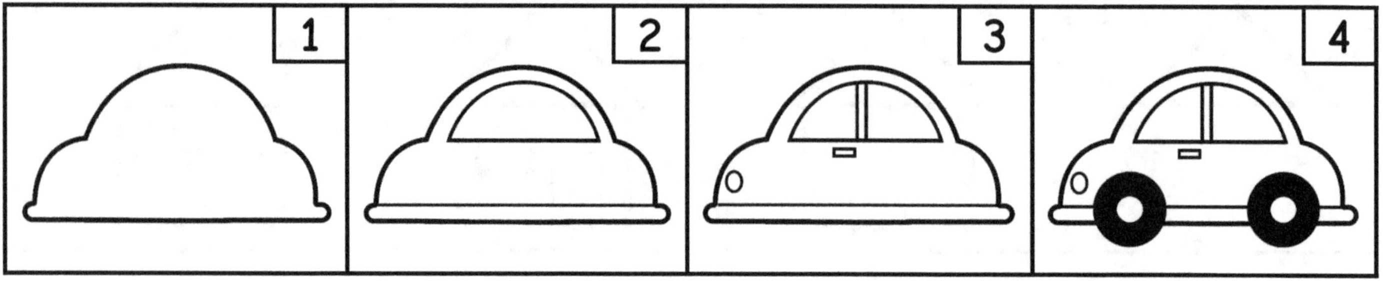

Skills: Drawing; Critical Thinking (Application)

Complete the hippopotamus.

Complete the flower.

Skills: Drawing; Symmetrical Thinking

Complete the starfish.

Complete the watermelon.

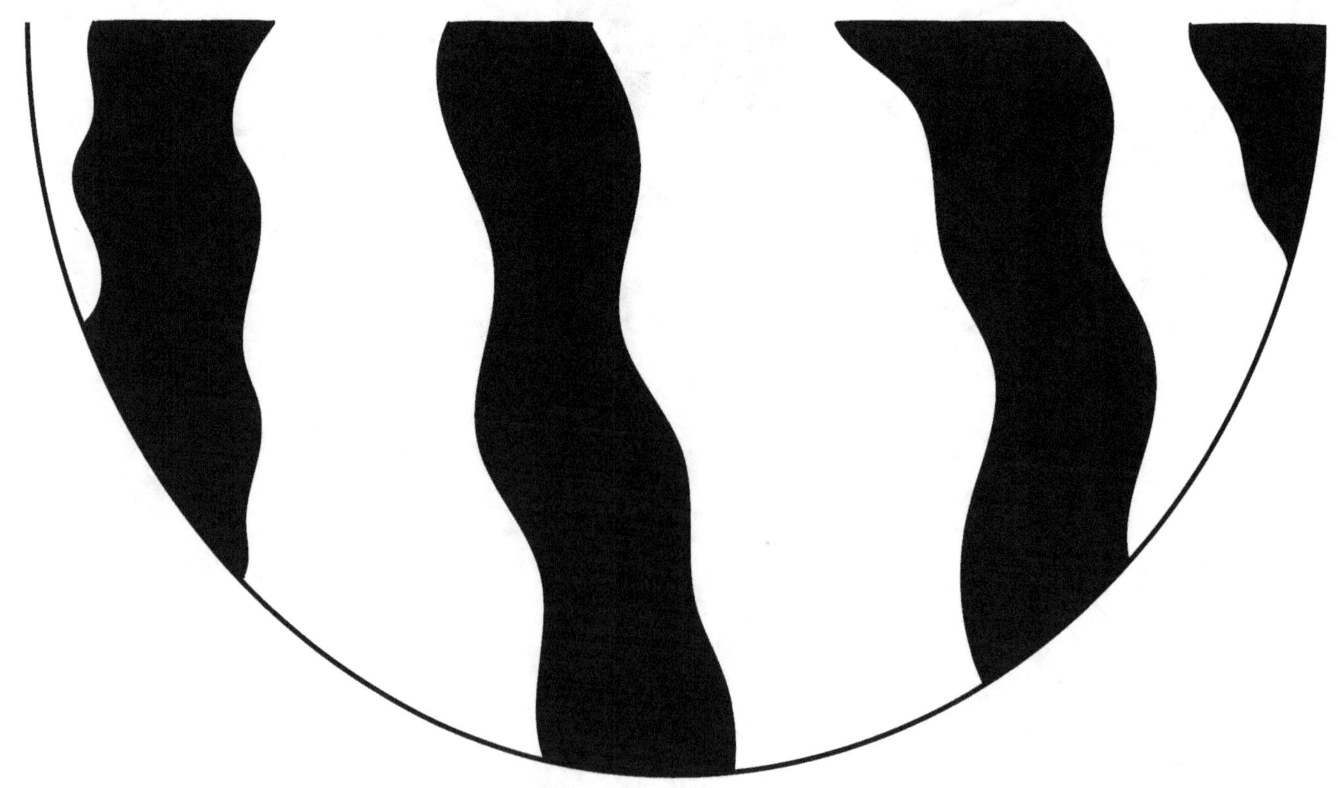

Skills: Drawing; Symmetrical Thinking

Art Application

Copy and draw on the grid.

Skills: Drawing; Critical Thinking (Application)

Art Application

Copy and draw on the grid.

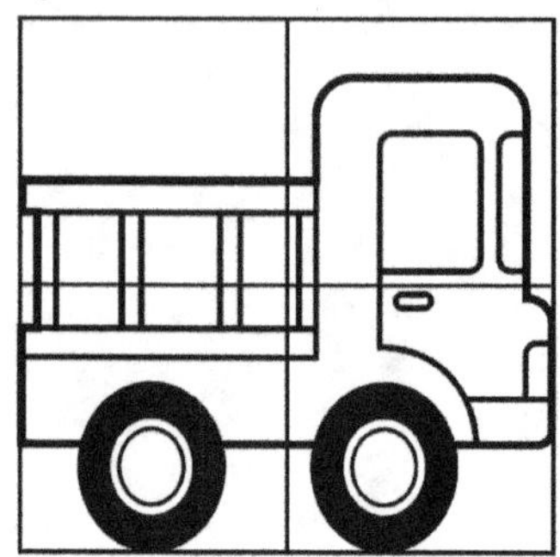

Skills: Drawing; Critical Thinking (Application)

Art Application

Use the code to color the picture.

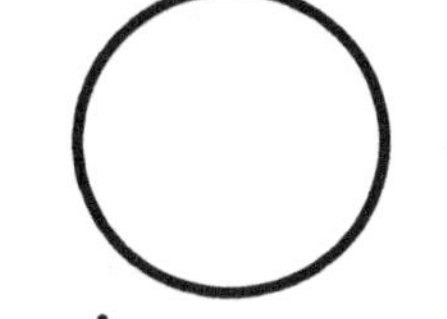
circle - green

triangle - red

square - yellow

rectangle - blue

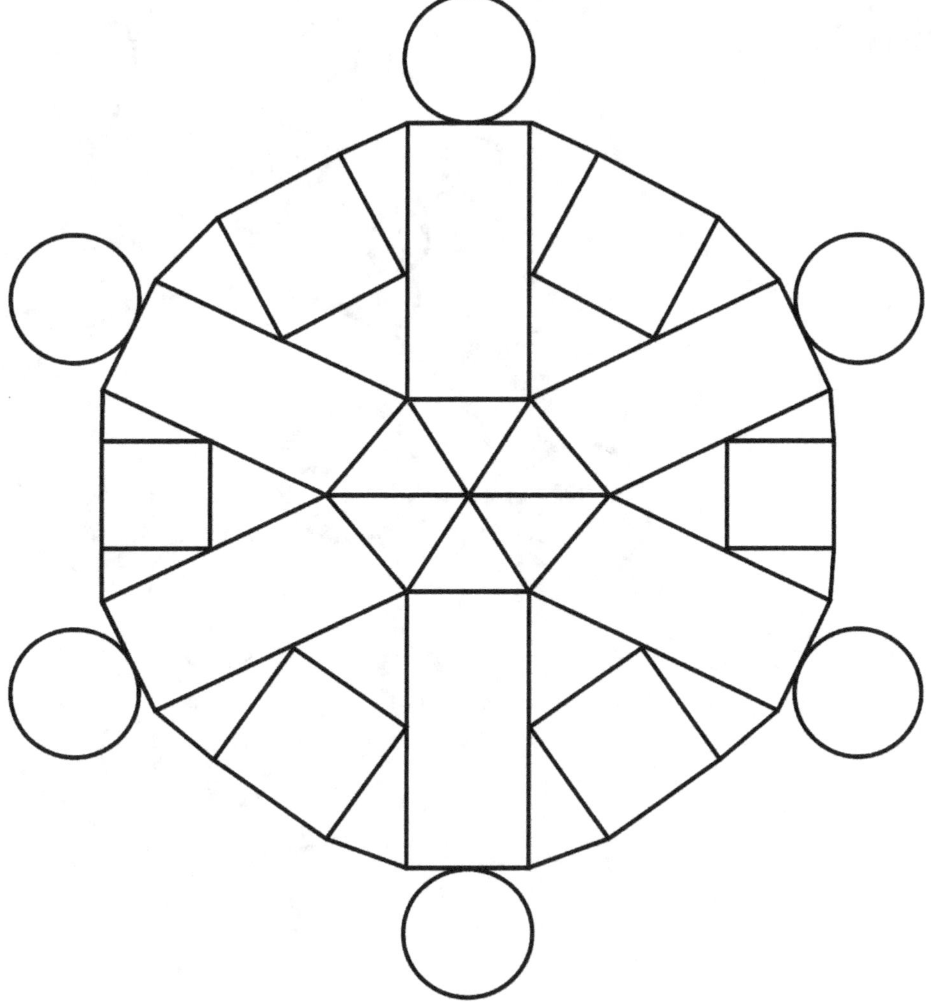

Art Application

Use the code to color the picture.

○ red

○ black

yellow

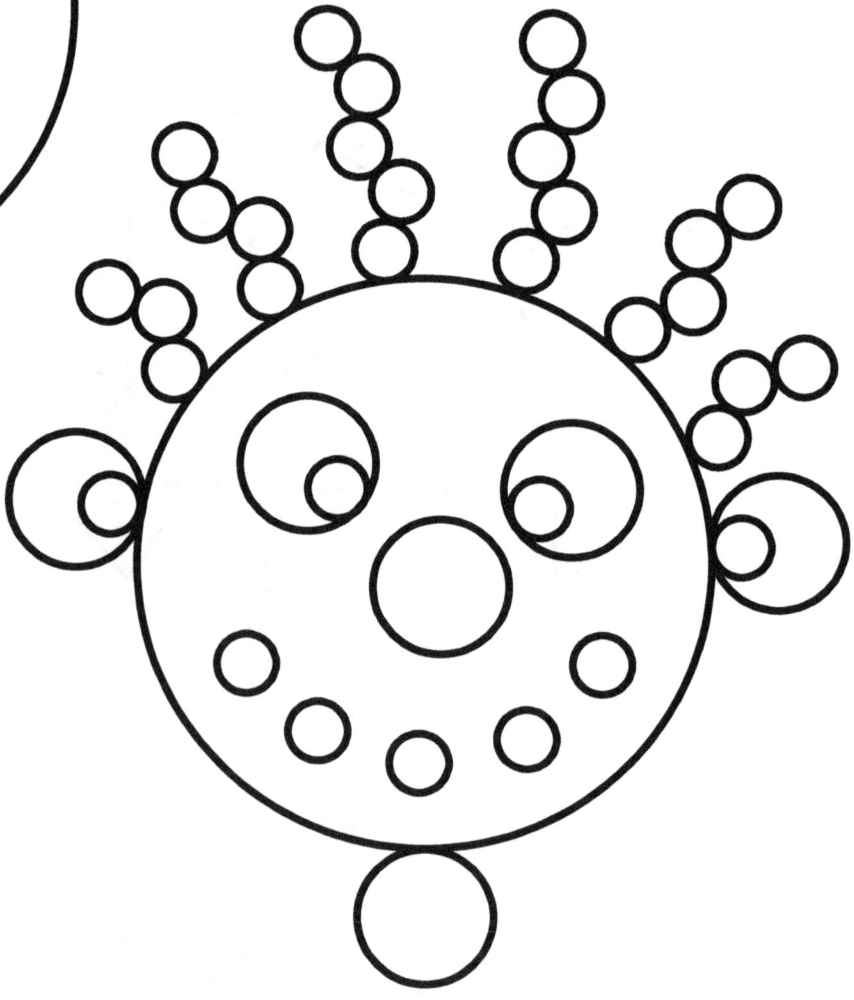

Skills: Coloring; Critical Thinking (Application)

Art Application

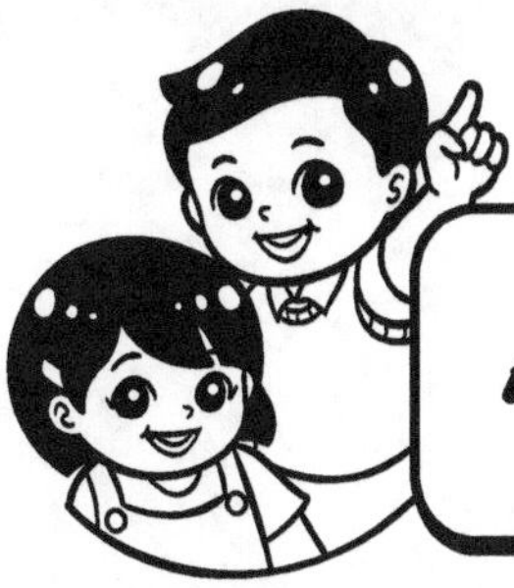

Color the pictures. Cut out the puzzle and form it on page 107. Glue the formed pieces on the page.

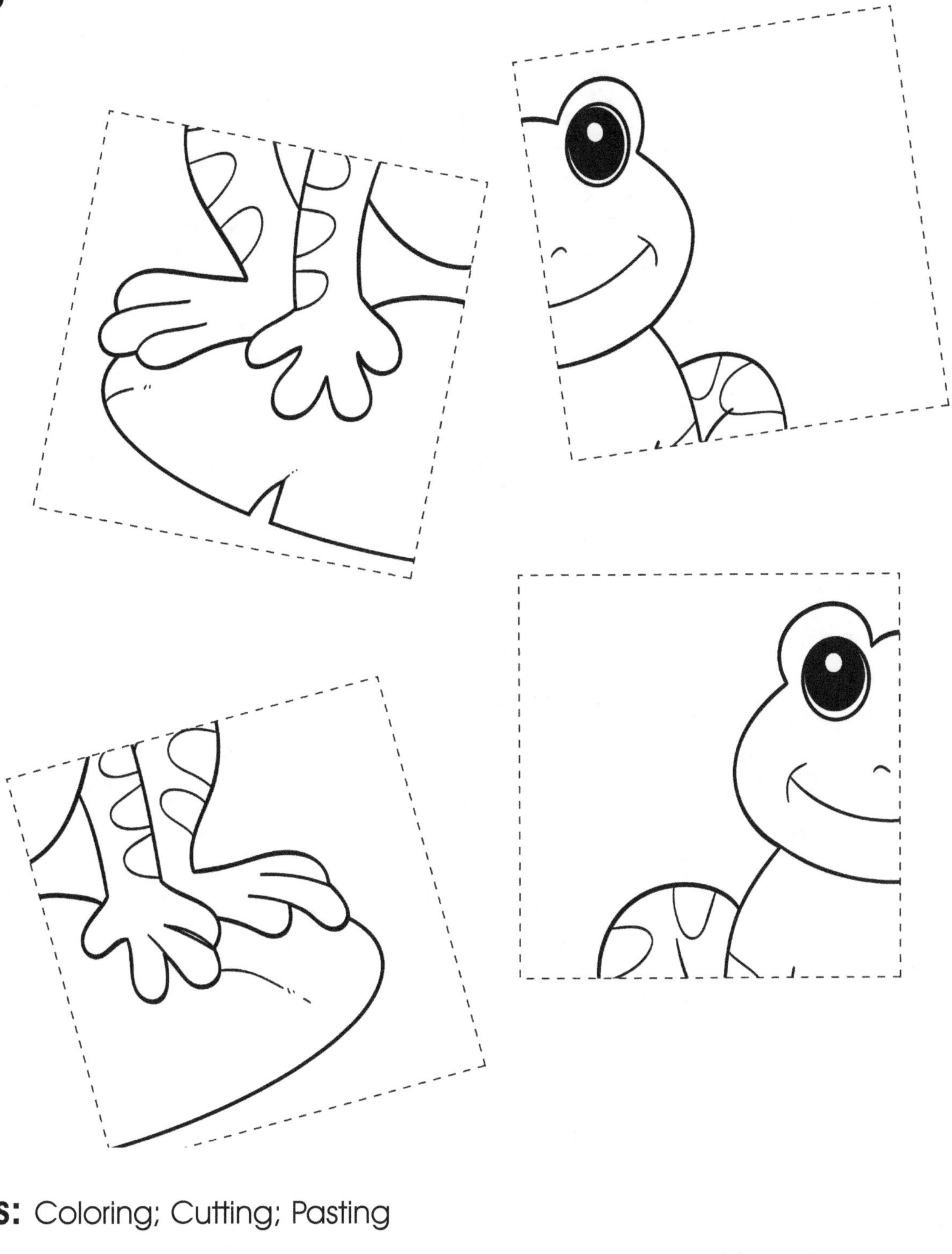

This is a frog.

PERFORMANCE TRACKER

Date	Lesson/Topic	Remarks
	Lines and Strokes	
	Shapes and Colors	
	Textures and Surfaces	
	Patterns and Styles	
	Special Occasions	
	Art Application	

Picture Books

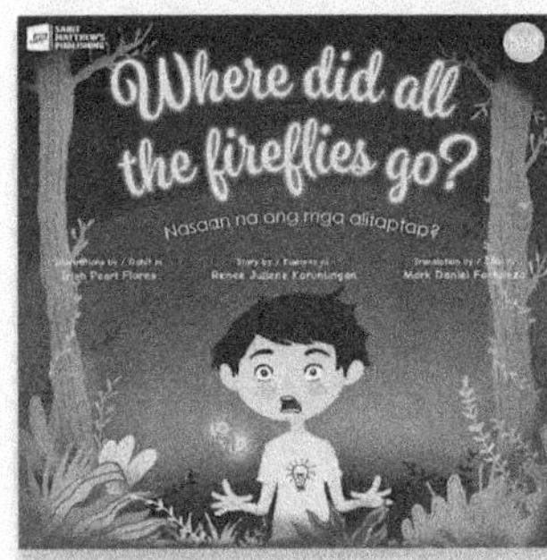

Bayani Biographies

Handy Books

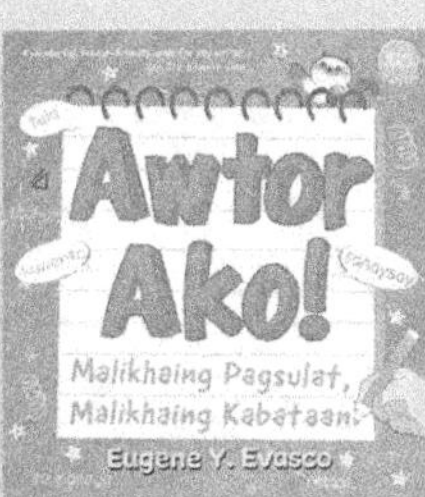

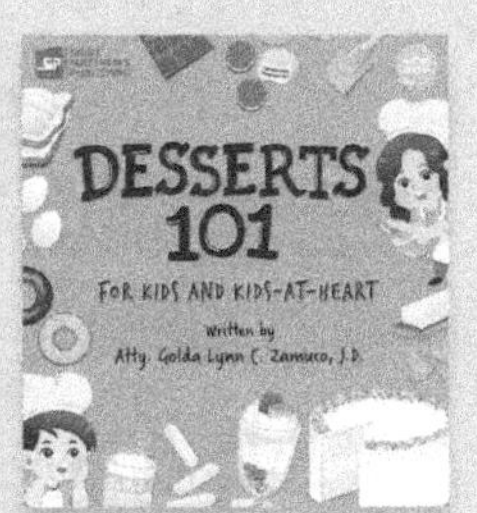

Purchase copies online!
www.stmatthews.ph

Kahel Press
is the children's book imprint of
St. Matthew's Publishing Corporation.

For inquiries and bulk orders
of children's books and textbooks,
contact us through
inquiry@stmatthews.ph
(02) 84265611.

www.ingramcontent.com/pod-product-compliance
Lightning Source LLC
Chambersburg PA
CBHW081256130726
47998CB00010B/2822